FOREX STRATEGIES

THE BEGINNER'S BIBLE TO MAKE SCALPING ON TRADING. FUNDAMENTALS FOR A GOOD MONEY MANAGEMENT SYSTEM MADE SIMPLE

By Tony Rental

©Copyright 2019 By Tony Rental

All rights reserved.

This document is geared towards providing exact and reliable information with regards to the topic and issue covered. The publication is sold with the idea that the publisher is not required to render accounting, officially permitted, or otherwise, qualified services. If advice is necessary, legal or professional, a practiced individual in the profession should be ordered.

From a Declaration of Principles which was accepted and approved equally by a Committee of the American Bar Association and a Committee of Publishers and Associations. In no way is it legal to reproduce, duplicate, or transmit any part of this document in either electronic means or in printed format. Recording of this publication is strictly prohibited and any storage of this document is not allowed unless with written permission from the publisher.

All rights reserved. The information provided herein is stated to be truthful and consistent, in that any liability, in terms of inattention or otherwise, by any usage or abuse of any policies, processes, or directions contained within is the solitary and utter responsibility of the recipient reader.

Under no circumstances will any legal responsibility or blame be held against the publisher for any reparation, damages, or monetary loss due to the information herein, either directly or indirectly. Respective authors own all copyrights not held by the publisher.

The information herein is offered for informational purposes solely, and is universal as so. The presentation of the information is without contract or any type of guarantee assurance.

The trademarks that are used are without any consent, and the publication of the trademark is without permission or backing by the trademark owner. All trademarks and brands within this book are for clarifying purposes only and are the owned by the owners themselves, not affiliated with this document

Table of Contents

INTRODUCTION

....

1

What exactly does Forex mean?

....

1

Which Forex Pairs Can You Trade?

....

2

Introduction to Forex - Major Currencies

....

4

Introduction to Forex - Concepts and Terminologies

....

7

How in particular Do Forex Quotes Work?

....

11

What is the Forex Spread? 13

What are Forex CFDs? 14

How Does Leverage Work in Forex Trading? 15

A Summary of Essential Forex Terms 16

What Are the Benefits of Forex Trading? 18

Why Trade FOREX? 20

Getting Started 29

A Variety of Leverage Options

31

Brokers That You Need to Avoid

33

Strict Margin Rules

34

Basic FOREX Strategy

35

Choosing Your Strategy

38

Understanding Forex Spreads

41

Successful Trading Tips

46

Forex Trading-- Rules of Thumb 55

Forex Trading Tools 70

   Analytics tools 71

Managing Your Money 78

   Forex Autopilot System (FAPS) 79

Forex: The World's Largest Financial Market 81

   Exchanging With A Demo Account 85

7 Questions to Ask to Find the Right Forex Broker
....
87

What to Look For in a Forex Trading Platform
....
95

Step by step instructions to Manage Your Risk When Trading Forex
....
100

Cash Management in Forex
....
105

Hazard Management Tools and Techniques
....
108

How to Analyse the Forex Market
....
112

6 Popular Forex Strategies

....

119

TYPES OF FINANCIAL MARKETS

....

122

Forex versus Futures

....

126

CONCLUSION

....

129

INTRODUCTION

Forex trading could be especially tough for newcomers. This may be mainly because the hopes of beginners are impractical. What you really need to say is that exchanging in currencies is certainly not really an achievement. On this section, you would get a description of the Forex market and even the rewards of trading in various currencies, how it functions and the primary jargon.

We will analyze how you would begin trading (including picking the best broker as well as trading software), the tenets of risks management, how you would evaluate the Forex market as well as a detailed analysis of the most popular commercial policies. You will still have the expertise to initiate the trial with a free demo profile before you join a live account as of the end of this section.

What exactly does Forex mean?

Forex seems to be the marketplace where currencies have been traded, or foreign exchange market (often named a brief FX). For instance, if you switch your domestic currency to something like a new one for an upcoming vacation a forex transaction might be easiest. The projected $5.3 billion has been exchanged among government bodies, financial institutions, businesses and investors daily all through the market in general.

It really is important to understand how well the market is established, because the team mixture of all actors establishes the market in which you exchange. The comparative mass of the marketing party is determined by the amount of funds the group uses from billions of dollars investment firms and financial institutions to some thousand dollars-deducted personal dealers.

Currencies were exchanged in sets and monetary pair organization measures the worth of one device vs. the other. The EURUSD monetary pair for instance analyses the value of the Euro especially in comparison to the US dollar. When the pair value goes up, the value of both the euro rises linked to the dollar's value. Whenever the duo's price reduces, united states dollar's value may have risen (or the euro's value is down).

Traders could still benefit from all these currency fluctuations via the trading of Foreign exchange and CFDs.

Which Forex Pairs Can You Trade?

Forex currency pairs are known as majors, minors, and exotics.

Major currency pairs are made up of the most frequently traded currencies, which are:

- USD - The US Dollar

- EUR - The Euro

- JPY - The Japanese Yen

- GBP - The British Pound

- CHF - The Swiss Franc

- CAD - The Canadian Dollar

- AUD - The Australian Dollar

- NZD - The New Zealand Dollar

A major currency pair is one that contains any one of these currencies paired against the US dollar, such as the EUR/USD, USDJPY or the GBPUSD. Forex minors pairs made up of these major currencies that don't include the US dollar. These pairs include EURGBP, EURCHF, AUDNZD and so on.

Finally, exotic currencies are any currencies that we haven't already mentioned, such as the Hong Kong Dollar (HKD), the Norwegian Krone (NOK), the South African Rand (ZAR) and the Thai Baht (THB). Exotic pairs include one exotic currency and one major currency.

When learning about Forex trading, many beginners tend to focus on major currency pairs because of their daily volatility and tight spreads. But there are numerous other opportunities – from exotic FX pairs, to CFD trading opportunities on stocks, commodities, energy futures, to indices. There are even indices that track groups of indices, and you can trade them as well.

How many markets you scan for opportunities is up to you, but do not limit yourself to just one instrument or one market. Market limitation can lead to overtrading, so make sure to diversify your investment.

Introduction to Forex - Major Currencies

a) The U.S. Dollar.

The United States dollar is the world's main currency – an universal measure to evaluate any other currency traded on

Forex. All currencies are generally quoted in U.S. dollar terms. Under conditions of international economic and political unrest, the U.S. dollar is the main safe-haven currency, which was proven particularly well during the Southeast Asian crisis of 1997-1998.

As it was indicated, the U.S. dollar became the leading currency toward the end of the Second World War along the Breton Woods Accord, as the other currencies were virtually pegged against it. The introduction of the euro in 1999 reduced the dollar's importance only marginally.

The other major currencies traded against the U.S. dollar are the euro, Japanese yen, British pound, and Swiss franc.

b) The Euro.

The euro was designed to become the premier currency in trading by simply being quoted in American terms. Like the U.S. dollar, the euro has a strong international presence stemming from members of the European Monetary Union. The currency remains lagued by unequal growth, high unemployment, and government resistance to structural changes. The pair was also weighed in 1999 and 2000 by outflows from foreign investors, particularly Japanese, who were forced to liquidate their losing investments in euro-denominated assets. Moreover, European money managers rebalanced their portfolios and reduced their euro exposure as their needs for hedging currency risk in Europe declined.

c) The Japanese Yen.

The Japanese yen is the third most traded currency in the world; it has a much smaller international presence than the U.S. dollar or the euro. The yen is very liquid around the world, practically around the clock. The natural demand to trade the yen concentrated mostly among the Japanese keiretsu, the economic and financial conglomerates. The yen is much more sensitive to the fortunes of the Nikkei index, the Japanese stock market, and the real estate market.

d) The British Pound.

Until the end of World War II, the pound was the currency of reference. The currency is heavily traded against the euro and the U.S. dollar, but has a spotty presence against other currencies. Prior to the introduction of the euro, both the pound benefited from any doubts about the currency convergence. After the introduction of the euro, Bank of England is attempting to bring the high U.K. rates closer to the lower rates in the euro zone. The pound could join the euro in the early 2000s, provided that the U.K. referendum is positive.

e) The Swiss Franc.

The Swiss franc is the only currency of a major European country that belongs neither to the European Monetary Union nor to the G-7 countries. Although the Swiss economy is relatively small, the Swiss franc is one of the four major currencies, closely resembling the strength and quality of the Swiss economy and finance. Switzerland has a very close economic relationship with Germany, and thus to the euro zone. Therefore, in terms of political uncertainty in the East, the Swiss franc is favored generally over the euro. Typically, it is believed that the Swiss franc is a stable currency. Actually, from a foreign exchange point of view, the Swiss franc closely resembles the patterns of the euro, but lacks its liquidity. As the demand for it exceeds supply, the Swiss franc can be more volatile than the euro.

Introduction to Forex - Concepts and Terminologies

Here are some important concepts/terminologies of Forex.

a) Spot rate

A spot transaction is a straightforward (or outright) exchange of one currency for another. The spot rate is the current market price or 'cash' rate. Spot transactions do not require immediate settlement, or payment 'on the spot'. By convention, the settlement date, or value date, is the second business day after the deal date on which the transaction is made by the two parties.

b) Bid & ask

In the foreign exchange market (and essentially in all markets) there is a buying and selling price. It is important to perceive these prices as a reflection of market condition.

A market maker is expected to quote simultaneously for his customers both a price at which he is willing to buy (the bid) and a price at which he is willing to sell (the ask) standard amounts of any currency for which he is making a market.

Generally, speaking the difference between the bid and ask rates reflect the level of liquidity in a certain instrument. On a normal trading day, the major currency pairs EURUSD, USDJPY, USDCHF and GBPUSD are traded by a multitude of market participant every few seconds. High liquidity means that there is always a seller for your buy and a buyer for your sell at actual prices.

c) Base currency and counter currency

Every foreign exchange transaction involves two currencies. It is important to keep straight which is the base currency and which is the counter currency. The counter currency is the numerator and the base currency is the denominator. When the counter currency increases, the base currency strengthens and becomes more expensive. When the counter currency decreases, the base currency weakens and becomes cheaper. In telephone trading communications, the base currency is always stated first. For example, a quotation for USDJPY means the US dollar is the base and the yen is the counter currency. In the case of GBPUSD (usually called 'cable') the British pound is the base and the US dollar is the counter currency.

d) Quotes in terms of base currency

Traders always think in terms of how much it costs to buy or sell the base currency. When a quote of 1.1750 / 53 is given that means that a trader can buy EUR against USD at 1.1753. If he is buying EURUSD for 1'000'000 at that rate he would have USD 1,175,300 in exchange for his million Euro. Of course traders are not actually interested in exchanging large amounts of different currency, their main focus is to buy at a low rate and sell at higher one.

e) Basis points or 'pips'

For most currencies, bid and offer quotes are carried down to the fourth decimal place. That represents one-hundredth of one percent, or 1/10,000th of the counter currency unit, usually called a 'pip'. However, for a few currency units that are relatively small in absolute value, such as the Japanese yen, quotes may be carried down to two decimal places and a 'pip' is 1/100th of the terms currency unit. In foreign exchange, a 'pip' is the smallest amount by which a price may fluctuate in that market.

f) Euro cross & cross rates

Euro cross rates are currency pairs that involve the Euro currency versus another currency. Examples of Euro crosses are EURJPY, EURCHF and GBPEUR. Currency pairs that involve neither the Euro nor the US dollar are called cross rates. Examples of cross rates are GBPJPY and CHFJPY. Of course hundreds of cross rates exist involving exotic currency pairs but they are often plagued by low liquidity. Ever since the Euro the number of liquid cross rates have decreased and have been replaced (to a certain extent) by Euro crosses.

How in particular Do Forex Quotes Work?

You can see both the' bid' and the' Ask' rates are quoted when you traded Forex. You will buy the currency at the bidding price, while the offer price is the cost of selling the currency. When you buy currency in an exchange, this is called a long-term business and the consolation is that the value of the currency pair will grow, so you can sell it at a higher price and make a your own profit from difference.

If you purchase a currency in a trading, the contrary is true-the consolation is that the currency pair will fall in and out of value, and you will be able to purchase it back at a lower cost.

The calculation for these prices is based on the current currencies trades in the pair or the exchange rate for a single unit of the first currency for the second currency (for example, if 1 EUR will have to be exchanged for 1,68 EUR, the offer and demand rates would be on both sides).

How Much Do Currency Values Change (Or, How Liquid Are Different Forex Pairs)?

If the way traders make a profit is by cashing in on the difference between the bid and ask prices of currency pairs, the next logical question is, how much can you expect any given currency to move?

This depends on how liquid the currency is, or how much of it is being bought and sold at any one time. The most liquid currency pairs are the ones with the most supply and demand in the Forex market, and this supply and demand is generated by banks, businesses, importers and exporters, and traders. Major currency pairs tend to be the most liquid, with the EUR/USD currency pair moving by 90-120 pips on an average day.

By contrast, the AUD/NZD moves by 50-60 pips a day, and the USDHKD currency pair only moves by an average of 32 pips a day (when looking at the value of currency pairs, most will be listed with five decimal points. A 'Pip' is 0.0001. So, if the EUR/USD moved from 1.16667 to 1.16677, that would represent a 1 pip change). The major Forex pairs tend to be the most liquid, and therefore provide the most opportunities for short-term trading.

However, there are many opportunities among minor and exotic currencies as well, particularly if you have some specialised knowledge about a certain currency.

What is the Forex Spread?

The spread, in Forex, is the distinction between the offer and solicit cost from a money pair. For instance, if the Bid cost of the EUR/USD is 1.16668, and the sell cost is 1.16669, the spread will be 0.0001, or 1 pip. In any Forex exchange, the estimation of a money pair should cross the spread before it gets gainful. To proceed with the past model, if a merchant entered a long EUR/USD exchange at 1.16668, the exchange wouldn't get beneficial until the estimation of the pair was higher than 1.16669.

In a money pair with a more extensive spread, for example, the EURCZK, the cash should make a bigger development all together for the exchange to get beneficial. At the hour of composing, the offer cost for this pair is 25.4373, while the ask cost is 25.4124, so the spread is 0.0200, or 20 pips. It's additionally normal for this cash pair to have developments of under 20 pips per day, which means dealers will probably need to play out a multi-day exchange to make a benefit.

This implies low-spread exchanging is frequently a need for Forex brokers, as their exchanges can get beneficial speedier, implying that they can make a high volume of littler exchanges, instead of depending on bigger exchanges to profit.

What are Forex CFDs?

In the event that you've been inquiring about Forex exchanging, you may have seen the term 'Forex CFDs' sooner or later. There are two different ways to exchange Forex: utilizing CFDs or spot Forex (otherwise called edge). Spot Forex includes purchasing and selling the genuine cash. For instance, you may buy a specific measure of Pound Sterling for Euros, and afterward, when the estimation of the Pound expands, you may then trade your Euros for Pounds once more, getting more cash back contrasted and what you initially spent on the buy.

The term CFD means 'Agreement For Difference', and it is an agreement used to speak to the development in the costs of money related instruments. As far as Forex, this implies instead of obtaining and selling a lot of money, you can benefit on value developments without owning the advantage itself. Alongside Forex, CFDs are additionally accessible on shares, lists, bonds, wares and digital forms of money. For each situation, they enable you to exchange on the value developments of these instruments without obtaining them.

Exchange With Admiral Markets

In case you're feeling roused to begin exchanging, or this BOOK has given some additional understanding to your current exchanging information, you might be satisfied to realize that Admiral Markets furnishes the capacity to exchange with Forex and CFDs on up to 80+ monetary standards, with the most recent market updates and specialized investigation accommodated FREE! Snap the standard underneath to open your live record today!

How Does Leverage Work in Forex Trading?

Alongside having the option to get to a wide scope of budgetary markets, another advantage of exchanging CFDs is that a broker can get to a lot bigger segment of those business sectors, and increment their potential benefits accordingly. CFD contracts give utilized access to the market, which means a broker can get to a lot bigger segment of the market than what they would have the option to buy by and large.

To utilize Gold CFD for instance, at the hour of composing, to buy an ounce of Gold you would need to burn through 1,200 USD. Be that as it may, with an influence pace of up to 1:20 (which implies a broker could exchange up to multiple times the estimation of what they store), a merchant could exchange on the full estimation of an ounce of gold (identical to 1,200 USD), for a store of only 60 USD.

Correspondingly, on the off chance that you needed to buy 3,000 USD with Euros, that would cost 2,570 EUR. With an influence pace of 1:30, in any case, you could get to 3,000 USD worth of the EUR/USD cash pair as a CFD with only 100 USD. The best part, notwithstanding, is that the size of the potential benefit a merchant could make is equivalent to on the off chance that they had put resources into the advantage out and out. The hazard here is that potential misfortunes are amplified to a similar degree as potential benefits.

A Summary of Essential Forex Terms

Before we proceed onward, we should recap a portion of the key ideas secured so far with this rundown of key Forex terms:

•   Pip: A pip is the base unit in the cost of cash sets, or 0.0001 of the provided cost estimate. So when the offer cost for the EUR/USD pair goes from 1.16667 to 1.16677, that speaks to a pip change of one.

•   Spread: The spread is the contrast between a cash pair's offered and ask cost. For the most famous money combines, the spread is regularly low - now and again even not exactly a pip! For sets that aren't exchanged as often as possible, the spread will in general be a lot higher. Before a Forex exchange gets beneficial, the estimation of the cash pair must cross the spread.

•   Margin: Margin is the cash in a dealer's record. Nonetheless, in light of the fact that the normal 'Retail Forex dealer' does not have the edge required to exchange a sufficiently high volume to make a decent benefit, numerous Forex and CFD representatives offer their customers access to use.

•   Leverage: Leverage is capital given by a Forex merchant to reinforce their customer's exchanging volume. For instance, in the event that you utilize a 1:10 pace of use and have $1,000 in your exchanging account, you can exchange $10,000 worth of a money pair. In the event that the exchange is effective, influence will expand your benefits by a factor of 10. In any case, if it's not too much trouble note that influence likewise increases your misfortunes to a similar degree, so it ought to be utilized with alert. On the off chance that your record balance falls beneath $0, you may trigger a representative's negative parity security settings (if exchanging with an ESMA directed dealer), which will bring about the exchange being shut. Luckily, this implies your parity can't move underneath $0, so you won't be owing debtors to the representative.

What Are the Benefits of Forex Trading?

Since we've shared a diagram of the Forex showcase, for what reason may you need to exchange Forex?

There are various reasons why individuals decide to begin day exchanging. A portion of these reasons may remember the possibility to win additional cash for the side from the solace of their own home, the chance to get familiar with another ability time permitting, or even the fantasy about accomplishing money related opportunity, and having more command over their budgetary future. With regards to Forex explicitly however, there are various advantages that make this budgetary instrument an alluring one to exchange.

On the off chance that you might want to become familiar with the contrasts between the Forex advertise and the Stocks showcase, why not look at our correlation article on the point? What's more, discover which market is directly for you! Forex Vs. Stocks: Should You Trade Forex or Stocks?

Why Trade FOREX?

The money/spot FOREX markets have certain novel qualities that offer an unequaled potential for gainful exchanging any economic situation or any phase of the business cycle. It leaves one to ask why trouble? The response to that is extremely basic.

It brags: A 24-hour market: A broker gets the opportunity to exploit the entirety of the gainful economic situations whenever which implies that there is no hanging tight for the 'opening ringer' like the trade.

Most noteworthy liquidity: The FOREX market is the most fluid market on the planet. That implies that a dealer can enter or leave the market at whatever point they need during practically any economic situation negligible execution boundaries or hazard and no every day exchanging limit.

High influence: An influence proportion of up to 400 is typical when contrasted with an influence proportion of 2 (half edge prerequisite) in the value markets. Obviously, this makes exchanging the money/spot forex showcase cumbersome a little since it makes the danger of the drawback misfortune a lot higher similarly that it makes the benefit potential on the upside a lot prettier.

Low exchange cost: The retail exchange cost (the offer/ask spread) is in reality under 0.1% (10 pips) under the typical economic situations. At bigger sellers, the spread could be under 5 pips, and may grow a lot in quick moving markets.

Continuously a buyer showcase: An exchange the FOREX market implies selling or getting one cash against another. Fundamentally, a positively trending business sector or a bear showcase for a cash is characterized as far as the standpoint for esteem against different monetary forms. In the event that the viewpoint is sure, you get a positively trending business sector where a merchant benefits by purchasing the money against different monetary forms. In any case, if the standpoint is negative, we have a positively trending business sector for different monetary forms and a broker benefits being compelled to selling the cash against other 10 monetary forms.

In either case, there is constantly a positively trending business sector exchanging open door for a merchant.

Between bank showcase: The establishment of the FOREX market comprises of a worldwide system of sellers that convey and exchange with their customers through electronic systems and phones. There are no sorted out trades like in fates that are there to fill in as a focal area to encourage exchanges the manner in which the New York Stock Exchange serves the value markets.

The FOREX market really works a ton like the manner in which the NASDAQ market in the United States works, and along these lines, it is additionally alluded to as an over the counter or OTC market.

Nobody can corner the market: The FOREX market is so enormous and has such a significant number of members that no single broker, even a national bank, can control the market cost for an all-inclusive timeframe. In any event, when mediations are led by strong national banks are getting the chance to be progressively insufficient and fleeting. This implies national banks are turning out to be less and less slanted to mediate to control market costs.

It is Unregulated: The FOREX market is viewed as an unregulated market despite the fact that the activities of significant sellers like business banks in cash focuses are managed under the financial laws.

The day by day activities of retail FOREX businesses are not managed under any laws or guidelines that are explicit to the FOREX market, and indeed, a significant number of these sorts of foundations in the United States don't answer to the Internal Revenue Service.

The money prospects and alternatives that are really exchanged on trades like Chicago 11 Mercantile Exchange (CME) are under the guideline in a similar way that other trade exchanged subsidiaries are directed.

There are a wide range of focal points to exchanging forex rather than stocks or futures, for example,

1. Lower Margin: Just like stocks and futures hypothesis, a forex broker can control a lot of the money essentially by setting up a limited quantity of margin.

Notwithstanding, the margin prerequisites that are required for exchanging prospects are typically around 5% of the full estimation of the holding, or half of the absolute estimation of the stocks, the margin necessities for forex is about 1%. For instance, edge required to exchange remote trade is $1000 for each $100,000.

This means exchanging forex, a cash merchant's cash can play with 5-times as a lot of estimation of item as a futures trader's, or multiple times in excess of a stock trader's.

At the point when you are exchanging on futures, this can be a truly beneficial approach to make a venture methodology, however it's significant that you require some investment to comprehend the dangers that are included too.

You should ensure that you completely see how your futures account is getting down to business. You will need to be certain that you read the edge understanding among you and your clearing firm. You will likewise need to converse with your record delegate on the off chance that you have any inquiries.

The places that you have in your record could be in part or totally exchanged on the opportunity that the accessible edge in your record falls beneath a foreordained sum.

You may not really get a margin call before your positions are sold.

Along these lines, you should screen your margin balance all the time and use stop-misfortune arranges on each vacant situation to restrict drawback chance.

2. No Commission and No Exchange Fees: When you exchange prospects, you need to pay trade and financier expenses.

Exchanging forex has the upside of being sans commission. This is obviously better for you. Money exchanging is an overall between bank showcase that lets purchasers to be coordinated with venders in a moment.

Despite the fact that you don't need to pay a commission charge to a representative to coordinate the purchaser with the vender, the spread is generally bigger than it is the point at which you are exchanging prospects.

For instance, on the off chance that you are exchanging a Japanese Yen/US Dollar pair, forex exchange would have around a 3 point spread (worth $30). Exchanging a JY futures exchange would in all likelihood have a spread of 1 point (worth $10) yet you would likewise be charged the intermediary's bonus. This cost could be as low as $10 in-and-out for self-coordinated internet exchanging, or as high as $50 for full-administration exchanging. It is comprehensive valuing however.

You will need to look at both online forex and your particular fates bonus charge to see which commission is the more prominent one.

3. Restricted Risk and Guaranteed Stops When you are exchanging fates, your hazard can be boundless. For instance, in the event that you felt that the costs for Live Cattle were going to proceed with their upward pattern in December 2003, just before the disclosure of Mad Cow Disease found in US cows.

The cost for it after that fell drastically, which moved the point of confinement during a few time in succession. You would not have had the option to leave your position and this could have cleared out the whole value in your record subsequently. As the value simply kept on 13 falling, you would have been committed to discover considerably more cash to make up the deficiency in your record.

4. Rollover of Positions When fates contracts terminate, you need to prepare in the event that you are going to rollover your exchanges. Forex positions terminate like clockwork and you have to rollover each exchange just with the goal that you can remain in your position.

5. 24-Hour Marketplace With prospects, you are for the most part constrained to exchanging just during the couple of hours that each market is open in any one day. On the off chance that a significant news story breaks out when the business sectors are shut, you won't have a method for receiving in return until the market revives, which could be numerous hours away.

Forex, then again, is a 24/5 market. The day starts in New York, and pursues the sun the world over through Europe, Asia, Australia and back to the US once more.

You can exchange whenever you like Monday-Friday.

6. Free commercial center Foreign trade is maybe the biggest market on the planet with a normal day by day volume of US$1.4 trillion. That is multiple times as huge as every one of the fates markets set up together! With the tremendous number of individuals exchanging forex around the world, it is hard for even governments to control the cost of their own money.

Forex exchanging is essentially an incredible option in contrast to fates and wares exchanging. Except if you are a representative, you will probably need to get some assistance in forex exchanging to help guarantee that your endeavor is fruitful. Similarly, as with all exchanging, there are in every case a few dangers included, yet in the event that you pursue this extensive to fruitful forex exchanging, the entire procedure ought to be a lot simpler. How about we begin!

• Forex is engaging by and large as a high-influence, high-hazard speculation condition where enormous scale benefits are conceivable in brief timeframes

• Forex is live for 24 hours per day, 5 days per week, leaving additional time and adaptability to exchange correlation with prospects or stocks • Risks can be limited with stop-misfortune rules and other comparable leave techniques.

Getting Started

When it comes to getting started in forex trading, there are quite a few things that you have to consider first. The first thing that you need to do is to find and choose the right broker to help you in making your trades.

When you are choosing a Broker you need to know that there are many FOREX brokers to choose from, just as in any other market. Here are some things that you need to look for in making your choice:

Low Spreads

The spread, which is calculated in pips, is the difference between the price at which a currency can be bought and the price at which it can be sold at any specific point in time. FOREX brokers don't charge a commission, so this difference is how they are going to make money.

When you are comparing brokers, you will find that the difference in spreads in FOREX is as large as the difference in commissions in the stock arena. What this means is that lower spreads will save you money and therefore, look for a broker that offers low spreads.

Quality of the Institution

Unlike equity brokers, FOREX brokers are usually attached to large banks or lending institutions because of the large amounts of capital that is required. Also, FOREX

brokers should be registered with the Futures Commission Merchant (FCM) as well as regulated by the Commodity Futures Trading Commission (CFTC).

You can find this and other financial information and statistics about a FOREX

brokerage on the company's website or the website of its parent company. You will want to make sure that your broker is backed by a reliable institution.

Extensive Tools and Research

FOREX brokers offer many different trading platforms for their clients just like brokers in other markets do. These different trading platforms often show real-time charts, technical analysis tools, real-time news and data, and even support for the various trading systems.

Before you commit to any one broker in specific, you will need to be sure to request free trials so that you can test their different trading platforms. Brokers usually provide technical as well as fundamental commentaries, economic calendars, and other research as a means of assisting you. Basically, you will want to find a broker who will give you everything that you need to succeed.

A Variety of Leverage Options

Leverage is a key necessity in FOREX trading because the price deviations (the sources of profit) are just set at mere fractions of a cent. Leverage, which is expressed as a ratio between total capitals that is available to actual capital, which is the amount of money a broker will lend you for trading.

For example, when you have a ratio of 100:1, this means that your broker would lend you $100 for every $1 of actual capital. Many brokerage firms will offer you as much as 250:1.

Of course, you need to remember that lower leverage also means lower risk of a margin call, but it also means that you will get a lower bang for your buck (and vice-versa). Basically if you have limited capital, you need to make sure that your broker offers high leverage.

If capital is not a problem, you can rest assured that any broker that has a wide variety of leverage options should suffice. A variety of options lets you vary the amount of risk you are willing to take. For example, less leverage (and therefore less risk) may be preferable if you are dealing with highly volatile (exotic) currency pairs.

Account Types

Many brokers will offer you two or more types of accounts. The smallest account is known as a mini account and it requires you to trade with a minimum of maybe $300.

This offers you a high amount of leverage (which you need in order to make money with so little initial capital). The standard account allows you to trade at a variety of different leverages, but it also requires a minimum initial capital of $2,000 to get you started.

Lastly, there are premium accounts, which often require significant amounts of capital to get you started. It also lets you use different amounts of leverage and often offer additional tools and services. You will need to make sure that the broker you choose has the right leverage, tools, and services that are relevant to the amount of capital that you are able to work with.

Brokers That You Need to Avoid

Just like there are brokers that you want, there are also brokers that you will want to stay away from. For example brokers who are prone to prematurely buying or selling near preset points (commonly referred to as sniping and hunting) are trifling things that are committed by brokers who only seek to increase profits.

Obviously, no broker would actually admit to doing this, but there are ways to know if a broker has committed this offense.

Unfortunately, the only way that you can really determine which brokers do this and which brokers don't is to talk to fellow traders. There is no actual list or organization that reports this kind of activity. The point here is that you have to talk to others in person or visit online discussion forums to find out who is an honest broker.

Strict Margin Rules

When you are trading with borrowed money, your broker should have a say in how much risk you are able to take. With this in mind, your broker can buy or sell at its discretion, which can be a really bad thing for you.

Let's just say that you have a margin account, and your position takes a headlong nosedive before it begins to rebound to all-time highs. Even if you have enough cash to cover it, some brokers will liquidate your position on a margin call at that low. This action on their part can cost you dearly. You talk to others in person or visit online discussion forums to find out who the honest brokers are.

Signing up for a FOREX account is a great deal like getting an equity account. The only major difference is that, for FOREX accounts, you are obligated to sign a margin agreement.

This agreement basically says that you are trading with borrowed money, and, 19

because of this the brokerage firm has the right to interfere with your trades in order to protect its interests. Once you sign up, all you have to do is fund your account and you'll be ready to trade right away.

Basic FOREX Strategy

Technical analysis and fundamental analysis are the two basic areas of strategy in the FOREX market which is the exact same as in the equity markets. However, technical analysis is by far the most common strategy that is used by individual FOREX traders. Here is a brief overview of both forms of analysis and how they directly apply to forex trading:

Fundamental Analysis

If you think it's hard enough to value one company, you should try valuing a whole country instead. Fundamental analysis in the forex market is often an extremely difficult one, and it's usually used only as a means to predict long-term trends.

However, it is important to mention that some traders do trade short term strictly on news releases. There are a lot of different fundamental indicators of the currency values released at many different times. Here are a few of them to get you started:

• Non-farm Payrolls

- Purchasing Managers Index (PMI)

- Consumer Price Index (CPI)

- Retail Sales

- Durable Goods

You need to know that these reports are not the only fundamental factors that you have to watch. There are also quite a variety of meetings where you can get some quotes and commentary that can affect markets just as much as any report. These meetings are often brought out to discuss any interest rates, inflation, and other issues that have the ability to affect currency values.

Even changes in how things are worded when addressing certain issues such as the 21

Federal Reserve chairman's comments on interest rates; can cause a volatile market.

Two important meetings that you have to watch out for are the Federal Open Market Committee and Humphrey Hawkins Hearings.

Just by reading the reports and examining the commentary, it can help FOREX fundamental analysts to get a better understanding of any and all long-term market trends and also to allow short-term traders to be able to profit from extraordinary happenings. If you do decide to follow a fundamental strategy, you will want to be sure to keep an economic calendar handy at all times so you know when these reports are released. Your broker may also be able to provide you with real-time access to this kind of information.

Technical Analysis

Just like their counterparts in the equity markets, technical analysts of the FOREX

trading market analyze price trends. The only real difference between technical analysis in FOREX and technical analysis in equities is the time frame that is involved in that FOREX markets are open 24 hours a day.

Because of this, some forms of technical analysis that factor in time have to be modified so that they can work with the 24 hour FOREX market. Some of the most common forms of technical analysis used in FOREX are:

- The Elliott Waves

- Fibonacci studies

- Parabolic SAR

- Pivot points

A lot of technical analysts have a tendency to combine technical studies to make more accurate predictions on your behalf. (The most common method for them is combining the Fibonacci studies with Elliott Waves.) Others prefer to create trading systems in an effort to repeatedly locate similar buying and selling conditions.

Using a profitable trading system with a demo account for a few weeks is a great way to get an accurate "feel" for Forex Trading – without risking any of your own money!

Choosing Your Strategy

Most successful traders will develop a strategy and perfect it over a specific period of time. Some people will focus on one particular study or calculation, while still some others use broad spectrum analysis as a means of determining their trades. Most experts would likely suggest that you try using a combination of both fundamental and technical analysis, with which you can make long-term projections and also determine entry and exit points. Of course, in the end, it is the individual trader who has to decide what works best for him.

When you are ready to get started in the FOREX market, you should open a demo

account and paper trade so that you can practice until you can make a consistent profit. Many people who fail have a tendency to jump into the FOREX market and quickly lose a lot of money because of a lack of experience. It is important to take your time and learn to trade properly before you start committing capital.

You also need to be able to trade without emotion. You can't keep track of all stop-loss points if you don't have the ability to execute them on time. You must always set your stop-loss and take-profit points to execute automatically, and don't change them unless you absolutely have to. Make your decisions and stick to them. Otherwise you will drive yourself (and your brokers) crazy.

You should also realize that you need to follow the trends. If you go against the trend, you are just messing with your money because the FOREX market tends to trend more often than anything else and you will have a higher chance of success in trading with the trend.

The FOREX market is the largest market in the world, and every day people are becoming increasingly interested in it. But before you begin trading, make sure your broker meets certain criteria, and take the time to find a trading strategy that works for you.

Understanding Forex Spreads

Forex is always priced in pairs between two different types of currencies. When you make a trade, you have to buy one currency and sell another at the same time. If you want to exit the trade, you must buy/sell the opposite position. For example, when you think the price of the Euro is going to rise against the US Dollar. In order for you to enter a trade, you will have to buy Euros and sell US Dollars.

If you want to leave the trade, you will have to sell Euros and buy back US Dollars.

You will be hoping that you were right in your guess and that the exchange rate for EU/USD has actually risen, which means that you will get more Euros back than when you bought them, which is how you will make a profit.

These days just about every forex broker is claiming to have the tightest spreads in the industry. But marketing does have the ability to be deceiving. The topic of spreads in the forex spot market is very complicated and often not easy to understand. However, nothing affects your trading profitability more.

Spreads are the biggest factor in your trading profits next to skill.

First of all, in order to understand the spread, you need to know what it is. A spread is the difference between the ask price (the price you buy at) and the bid price (the price you sell at) that is quoted in the pips. If the quote between EUR/USD at a given moment is 1.2222/4, then the spread equals 2 pips. If the quote is 1.22225/40, then the spread is going to equal 1.5 pips.

The spread is how brokers make their money. Wider spreads will result in a higher asking price and a lower bid price. The consequence to this is that you have to pay more when you buy and get less when you sell, which makes it more difficult to realize a profit

Brokers generally don't earn the full spread, especially when they hedge client positions. The spread helps to compensate for the market maker for taking on risk from the time it starts a client trade to when the broker's net exposure is hedged (which could possibly be at a different price).

Spreads are important because they affect the return on your trading strategy in a big way. As a trader, your sole interest is buying low and selling high (like futures and commodities trading). Wider spreads means buying higher and having to sell lower. A half-pip lower spread doesn't necessarily sound like much, but it can easily mean the difference between a profitable trading strategy and one that isn't profitable.

The tighter the spread is the better things are going to be for you. However tight spreads are only meaningful when they are paired up with good execution. Quality of execution will decide whether you actually receive tight spreads. A good example of this is when your screen shows a tight spread, but your trade is filled a few pips to your disadvantage or is mysteriously rejected.

When this occurs repeatedly, it means that your broker is showing tight spreads but is effectively delivering wider spreads. Rejected trades, delayed execution, slipping, and stop-hunting are strategies that some brokers use to get rid of the promise of tight spreads.

Spreads should always be considered in conjunction with depth of book. Oddly enough, when it comes to economies of scale, forex doesn't even act like most other markets. On the inter-bank market, for example; the larger the ticket size, the larger the spread is. So when you see a 1-pip spread on an ECN platform, you have to wonder if that spread valid for a $2M, $5M or $10M trade, which it probably isn't. In many cases, the tight spread that is offered applies only to a capped trade sizes that are very inadequate for most of the common trading strategies.

Spread policies change a great deal from broker to broker, and the policies are often 27

difficult to see through. This certainly makes comparing brokers much more difficult.

Some brokers actually offer fixed spreads that are guaranteed to remain the same regardless of market liquidity. But since fixed spreads are traditionally higher than average variable spreads, you are paying an insurance premium during most of the trading day so that you can get protection from short-term volatility.

Other brokers offer traders variable spreads depending on market liquidity. Spreads are tighter when there is good market liquidity but they will widen as liquidity dries up. When it comes to choosing between fixed and variable rates, the choice depends on your individual trading pattern. If you trade primarily on news announcements that you hear, you may be better off with fixed spreads. But only if quality of execution is good.

Some brokers have different spreads for different clients based on their accounts. For example; those clients that have larger accounts or those who make larger trades may receive tighter spreads, while the clients that are referred by an introducing broker might receive wider spreads in order to cover the costs of the referral. Some offer the same spreads to everyone.

Problems can come up when you are trying to learn about a company's spread policy because this information, along with information on trade execution and order-book depth is rather difficult to get. Because of this, many traders get caught up in all of the promises they hear, and take a broker's words at face value. This can be dangerous. The only real way to find out is to try out various brokers or talk to those who have.

Successful Trading Tips

There is no doubt that trading requires more than a few quick tips for success.

You need experience, fortitude, capital and, above all, a solid trading system.

However, for the average beginner and those who perhaps are losing their focus because of significant draw-downs, keeping things simple can help to introduce much needed focus into your trading.

To that end, here are some tips that you can use for trading that can help you get a handle on these exciting markets:

1. Never add to a position that is losing.

2. Always determine a stop and a profit objective before you start entering a trade. Place stops that are based on market information, and not your account balance. If a "proper" stop is too expensive, it isn't worth it to make the trade.

3. Remember the power of a position. You should never make a market judgment when you have a position.

4. Your decision to exit a trade means that you are able to perceive changing circumstances. You shouldn't think you can pick a price, exit at the market.

5. In a Bull market, you never want to sell a dull market, in Bear market, you should certainly never buy a dull market.

6. There are times, due to a lack of liquidity, or excessive volatility, when you should not trade at all.

7. Trading systems that work in an up market may not work in a down market. It is good to know this and remember it.

8. There are at least three types of markets like up trending, range bound, and down trading, and you should have a different trading strategy for each.

9. Up market and down market patterns are ALWAYS there, and it is only that one is always more dominant. In an up market, for example, it is very easy to take sell signal after sell signal, only to be stopped repeatedly. Select trades that move along with the trend.

10. A buy signal that fails is really just a sell signal. A sell signal that fails is a buy signal.

11. It's always easier to enter a losing trade.

12. During the blowout stage of the market, up or down, the risk managers are usually issuing margin call position liquidation orders. They don't generally check the screen for overbought or oversold; they just keep issuing liquidation orders. It is best to make sure that you don't stand in the way.

13. It's good to be superstitious; in that you shouldn't trade if something bothers you.

14. Buy the news that you hear, sell the factual news.

15. News is only important when the market doesn't react in the direction of the news.

16. It helps for you to read today's paper tomorrow. When you read yesterday's paper each day with the knowledge of what the market already did, it will remind you that what happened yesterday has nothing to do with what will happen today.

17. You should never enter a new trade in the direction of a gap. Never let the market make you make a trade.

18. The first and last tick are always the most expensive. Get in late and out early.

19. When everyone else is in, it's time for you to get out.

20. Never trade when you are sick.

21. You should only change your unit of trading under a plan of attained goals. You should also have a plan for reducing size when your trading is cold or market volume is down.

22. Confidence is a bad thing. Remember, you really don't know anything unless you are a broker. You need to expect the unexpected. Always know your position and exit your trade immediately whenever you feel uneasy.

23. Measure yourself by profitable consecutive days and not by individual trades.

24. The best way to break a streak of consecutive loses is to not trade for a day.

25. Don't stop trading when you're on a 'winning streak'. At the same time, however, stick to your stop-loss rules and money-management strategy, and don't think that luck has anything to

do with it. Your trading system may simply be having an optimal time-period.

26. Don't turn three losing trades in a row into six in a row. When you're off, turn off the screen, do something else. Sticking in when you are loosing is just silly.

27. Scalpers reduce the number of variables effecting market risk by being in a position only for a few seconds. Day traders reduce market risk by being in trades for minutes.

28. If you convert a scalp or day trade into a position trade, technically you did not consider the risks of the trade properly.

29. You should not worry about a missed opportunity. There is always another one just around the corner.

30. If you look for secrets in the market you will only find things that no one cares about. It is better to use the tools, which will be covered in the next section.

31. Never ask for someone else's opinion, they probably did not do as much homework as you did anyways.

32. When the market is going up, you should say it aloud. When the market is going down, you want to say that aloud too. The reason for this is that you'd be amazed at how hard it is to say what is literally going on in front of you when your mind is full of preconceived opinions.

33. Successful day trading requires flexibility. You have to do your homework so that you can understand the full potential for both sides of the market. This will allow you to make your trades based on what the market is doing at the time of the trade.

34. Here is a quote that would be good for you to remember: "When you wake up, your instincts are wrong."

35. When you make a mistake of discipline, whine like a fool to anyone that will listen. Any errors that are made in discipline are mistakes you will keep on making for many years. Wearing ashes and sack cloth may help you to extend the time before you do it again.

36. If you whined or got fidgety while you read this list, then you share two obvious characteristics with many other traders:

A. You have traded long enough to recognize that you (not the market) make mistakes, and you try to overcome them.

B. This fact is awkward, you have become part of the market and you can never leave. No matter where life takes you, you will always check the market and you will also always want to continue being a part of it.

1. For small accounts ($25,000 and under), like I said before you need to trade with the trend. Many beginners look for trades that flow in any direction.

While forex trading easily permits bi-directional trading, trading in the direction of the trend improves your odds over the long run.

2. You should have at least two accounts. One real account and the other a demo account. Learning doesn't stop when trading real dollars begins. Keep the demo account and use it to test any alternative trades etc. For example, you can shadow your real trades with identical ones in your demo account, but you will want to widen your stops in the demo in an effort to see if you're being too conservative.

3. You have to stop looking for leading indicators because there aren't any.

While some firms make a lot of money selling software that predicts the future, the reality is that if those products really worked, they wouldn't be telling you about it.

4. Examine the daily charts, the four-hour charts and one-hour charts are there to assist you in timing your trades. While you are trading at 30- and 15-minute time increments, it takes a great deal of dexterity.

5. Don't trade the time frame that is offered. Trade the pattern instead.

Reversal patterns, hesitation patterns and breakout patterns show up a lot.

Learn to look for the pattern in any time frame.

6. If you have the right amount of money, trading two lots is safer than just trading one. Trading three lots is safer than two etc. Trading is a big pile of emotions, technical analysis and money management. One lot alone makes it difficult to weigh these elements in deciding to enter or exit.

7. Extreme trading can be the most conservative trading when you think about it. Trading at the extremes increases the odds that you have chosen the right direction.

8. You should fully check the Big Five the dollar/yen, euro/dollar, Swiss franc/

dollar, euro/yen and pound/dollar before you decide to take a position in any one of them. There might be something obvious that you've missed.

9. Follow the Upside Down Rule. If you can turn a chart upside down and it still looks the same, avoid it all together.

10. Don't keep count of your profits in your first 20 trades. Keep track of the

percentage of wins instead. Once you know you can pick direction, profits can be increased with multi-plot trading and by using variations in your stops. In other words, now is the time to get serious about your personal money management.

Forex Trading-- Rules of Thumb

In this section we will be covering the few important rules that should never be broken in trading. If you can apply these rules consistently, and with the right amount of discipline, you will be well on the way to being a profitable trader. The following are rules that can significantly improve your chances of success if they are understood, practiced, and implemented consistently in your trading. These rules have been learned the hard way, mostly through trial-and-error, and the inevitable mistakes that everyone makes when they start a trading business.

Set up and Implement specific goals and objectives

Few things are more important to your trading success than having set specific goals and objectives for what you are trying to achieve. It is amazing to me how often we hit our targets, meet our objectives, and reach our goals best when we speak aloud and write them down.

For any business to be successful it must have measurable objectives that you are actually able to achievable. In trading, the primary objective is obviously to make money, but it is important to have other objectives that are not strictly cash-related.

We must always remember that reward and risk go hand-in-hand in trading and that we can't expect to achieve high returns without planning and bracing for high risk (draw-downs).

Your objectives and goals have to be very specific to you, but they must also include the following characteristics if they are going to be useful:

• Be measurable in accordance to completion and timeframe involved

• Be realistic and achievable

• Be worth the time and effort involved

• Be positive

As an example, here are some actual objectives (Please bear in mind that this is only a partial list):

• Create 2 new positive-expectancy trading systems each and every year

• Seek to make less errors implementing your trading systems each year

• Work to achieve a return to maximum draw-down ratio of 1.5:1

- Take 2 weeks vacation from trading during each year

You should also note that only one of them is meant to be about making money, and that has a measurable objective that is very similar to a draw-down, and it is not guaranteed. If you know what you are trying to gain in your trading, and when you are trying to achieve it, the whole of your efforts will be more focused on meeting your objectives.

This also helps to guide you to only pay attention to things you really want to achieve with your time and resources that you have available. This will also give you a way that you can effectively measure the success and progress of your trading strategy.

Generally, traders who have well-defined objectives will be much more successful than those that do not have pre-defined goals.

Consistency and discipline

In order for you to be able to realize the full potential of your trading systems it is very important that you take every trading entry, adjust every stop, and close out every trade when your pre-defined trading system says you should.

This takes an extreme amount of confidence in your trading systems, good and reliable technology, and the unwavering discipline to stick to your trading plan no matter what happens.

The good thing about have an underlying assumption about being consistent and disciplined is that you have a pre-defined plan for every situation that you may face in your trading, so that you know how you are defining what being consistent really means. Your plan needs to include at least the following items in it if it is going to be successful:

• All of your trading rules for entering, adding to, and getting out of your positions

• What you are planning to do if your trading computer, internet connection, broker, power, telephone etc. fails to be of any real use or break down

• What you will do if for some reason you are unable to trade

• What you will do if you lose a certain percentage of your account

• What you will do if all the markets are closed and you can't get out of your current positions

Unless you write down the answers to all these scenarios, you cannot be properly consistent and disciplined in your approach to trading and if you lose money you will not know if it is because you didn't follow your plan, your plan is incomplete, your systems do not work, or if it is because you are simply going through a losing period.

Let your profits run

This rule is undoubtedly the key to being a successful trader. It is in these three simple words however that are easier said than done. When we get a profitable trade going it is our natural fear of losing the unrealized cash starts and we truly want to close it out now and quit while we are ahead.

Most trading actually consists of long periods of small winners and losers, that is quickly followed by a few huge winners that make the difference between overall profitability and simply breaking even or even losing thanks to the trading costs (commissions, spread, and slippage).

It is our ability to let the huge winners become huge. This is what determines how we will perform overall during the course of the year. The key here is in letting a winning streak run is to have trailing stops that are generally outside the daily noise of the market so that they are not so tight as to get stopped out during 'normal' trading process.

This means that you need to be prepared to give up a relatively large portion of a winning trade's open profit and it is also the thing that makes this so hard to implement. In fact, we should be adding to a winner and widening stops rather than trying to figure out how tight our stops can be to capture the largest amount of profit.

The trade has already shown you if it intends to be a winner, and the chances are it is a low-risk idea if you were to add to the position now rather than 'strangle it' with stops that are too tight.

It is very important that your management rules leave room for large winning trades, and that the rules are pre-defined and understood before you place the trade in the first place. This will allow you to stick to your rules when you do get the big winner.

Cut your losses short

This is actually the sister rule to the one mentioned above, and is usually just as difficult to do (even if it is very easy to define). In the same way that profitability comes from a few large winning trades, capital preservation so comes from avoiding the few large losers that the market will see fit to send you each year.

Setting a maximum loss point before you enter the trade so you know ahead of time approximately how much you are risking on this position is pretty straight up.

You just have to have an exit price that tells you that your trade is a losing one you should exit before it gets any bigger. Because of gaps at the open, or limit moves in futures we can never be 100% sure that we can get out with our maximum loss, but simply having the rules, and always sticking to them will save us from the nasty trades that just keep on going against our position until we have lost more than many winning trades can make back.

If you have a losing position that is at your maximum loss point, you should just get out right away. You can't hope that it will turn around for as it isn't common sense.

Being that trades are either winners or losers, and this one is shouting 'Loser' at you, the chances that it will turn around and become a large winner is decidedly small.

Why would you want to risk any more money on a trade that has already shown itself to be a loser when you could simply close it out (accept the loss) and move on. This will leave you in a much better place financially and mentally, than holding on to your position and hoping it will go back your way.

Even if it did do this, the mental energy and negative feelings from holding the losing position are just not worth it. this is why you should always stick to your rules and exit a position if it hits your stop point.

Never add to a losing trade

One of the few trade management rules that you should never break is 'Never add to a losing trade'. Trades are split into winners and losers, and if a trade is a loser, the chances of it turning right around and becoming a winner are too small for you to want to risk more money on. If it actually is a winner disguised as a loser, why not wait until it shows it is a winner before you add to it.

If you do this you will notice that nearly every time the trade ends up hitting your 40

stop loss and does not change direction. Sometimes the trade turns around before it hits your stop and becomes a winner and you can count yourself very lucky if it does.

Sometimes the trade hits your stop loss and then turns around and becomes a winner and you can count yourself unlucky. Whatever happens, it is never worth adding to a loser, hoping that it will eventually be a winner. The odds of success are just too low to risk more capital in addition to the initial risk.

Don't take too much risk

One of the most devastating mistakes that any trader can make is in risking too much of their capital on a single trade. One thing is certain in trading and that is if you lose all your capital you are out of the game indefinitely. Why should you risk so much when you could be prevented from continuing?

There is a useful saying in poker than going all-in works every time but once. It is the same thing in trading. If you risk all of your account on every trade it only takes one loser to wipe you out, so you will be out of the game at some point as it is only a question of time.

In general, you should only risk 1-3% of the available capital allocated to a system on any individual trade. This is calculated using the size and, the difference between our entry price and our maximum stop price, and the amount of capital that is allocated to the system.

With these things combined we are almost certain never to lose all of our trading capital. In fact, the chance of us hitting our maximum drawdown for the year is extremely low.

All trades that you make should be of a size that almost seems pointless to your future fortune. If you are worried about the size of a trade then it is too big and you should use a lower amount immediately.

Remember that longevity in any trading market is the key to making money by trading. You should trade slowly over a long time with minimal risk, is always preferable to rapidly with too much risk.

Only trade positive expectancy systems

If you have a positive expectancy trading system, the only factors that will decide how much money you will make per year are the number of trades the system actually makes, how much capital you allocate to the system, and how accurately you use the trading signals.

If you do not know whether your trading system is positive expectancy then it makes no sense for you to be trading it in the first place. Expectancy is calculated using the profit or loss on each trade; divided by the initial risk, and then taking the average of this number of a series of trades. Systems that have positive expectancy will make money most of the time and those with negative expectancy will lose money.

Successful traders only trade systems when the odds of success are in their favor so that they know that making money is the final result of accurately implementing the system and not just pure luck.

You will want to minimize all of you trading business costs Some trading systems can offer you only marginal profitability, and trading implementation costs (commission, spread, and slippage) can be the difference between making a profit and making a loss.

With the simple availability of modern electronic brokers, and fully-automated trade processing and execution, it is definitely worth the effort in looking for a very low cost way to implement your trading system.

High commission, wide spreads, and large amounts of slippage can be lowered drastically and easily by carefully choosing the right broker. This can be the difference between a system being useable or not. Paying too much for trade implementation is a way to lose money that you can actually avoid.

For those just starting out, we recommend Easy Forex as a broker/platform due to their relatively affordable spreads and fee structure.

Educate yourself

In order for you to be able to compete at the highest level in the trading business and be a successful player, you must be well-educated about what you are doing. Being well-educated means that you have thoroughly researched and tested your trading ideas and know why your trading system worked in the past and is still working.

It means that you understand all the technology and applications that your system needs to perform with accuracy. It means understanding your goal and objectives and how trading will help you achieve them. It means understanding yourself and how your personality will affect your results.

In order to succeed as a forex trader, you really need to become an expert in your own trading business to understand how it the dots are all connected, when it is broken, and how it can be improved. This takes commitment, hard work, dedication, and more hard work.

Avoid trading scared money

No one ever made any money trading when they had to do it to pay their bills at the end of the month. Having a requirement to make a certain amount of dollars per month or you will be financially in trouble is the best way I know to completely mess up all trading discipline, rules, objectives, and leads faster than you'd expect to disaster.

Trading is about taking a reasonable amount of risk in order to achieve a good reward.

The markets and how and when they give up their profits is nothing that you can control. You should never trade if you need the money to pay bills. Do not trade if your business and personal expenses are not covered by another income stream or cash reserve. This is how hasty decisions are made.

The one proven method to keeping your losses small is to set your maximum loss before you even open a Forex trading position.

The maximum loss is the greatest amount of capital that you are comfortable losing on any one trade. With your maximum loss set as a small percentage of your Forex trading effort, a string of losses won't stop you from trading for any particular amount of time. Unlike the 95% of Forex traders out there who lose money because they haven't implemented wise money management rules to their Forex trading system, you will be ok with this money management rule.

To use as an example- If I had a Forex trading float of $2000, and I began trading with $200 a trade, it would be reasonable for me to experience three losses in a row. This would reduce my Forex trading capital to $800. It would then be decided that they're going to bet $400 on the next trade because they think they have a higher chance of winning after having lost three times already.

If that trader did bet $200 dollars on the next trade because they thought they were going to win, their capital could be reduced to $500 dollars. The chances of making money now are practically nil because I would need to make 150% on the next trade just to break even. If the maximum loss had been determined, and stuck to, they would not be in this position.

In this case, the reason for failure was because the trader risked too much money, and didn't apply good money management to the play.

Remember, the goal here is to keep our losses as small as possible while also making sure that we open a large enough position to capitalize on profits and minimize losses. With your money management rules in place, in your Forex trading system, you will always be able to do this.

Forex Trading Tools

When it comes to getting started with forex trading, the tools that you should get will certainly make learning and executing your trading efforts a great deal easier. Just like you would calculator before you bought a house, there are special tools that you can use when trading forex as well.

Below you will find a list and descriptions of some of the popular tools that are used to help you make your trading experience easier. They are listed in terms of what they do as well. Let's look at these right now!

Automatic Execution tool

The Advanz Auto4X platform helps to take your Trade Station strategy signals and also automates their execution to Gain Capital's trading platform. Advanz Auto4X is designed so that it can be powerful, flexible and accurate so as to meet the needs of various complex institutional trading departments.

It is also designed to be simple and efficient for an individual trader. Advanz Auto4X also helps to support the execution of a variety of different strategies working on any number of time frames to all of the Forex crosses that are made available for trading.

Analytics tools

Elliott Wave

This is considered by most experienced traders to be the purest form for getting technical analysis because Elliott Wave analysis measures investor psychology. The Wave reveals that mass psychological swings during a natural sequence, which creates specific and measurable patterns.

This actually offers you daily technical analysis and trading recommendations that are based on sophisticated trading K.B. Advisory Ltd.

TRL is a Specialist Foreign Exchange Forecasting Service that can help you with forecasting and trading analysis in the (Technical Research global foreign exchange markets. Technical Research Limited Limited) is rated the No. 1 FX Advisory Service by customers in 39 different countries around the world.

This program is very powerful, and offers you real-time analysis for market professionals who are looking for:

1. An edge with decision making support

2. Top performing market models

3. To spend less $$ on real-time data and exchange feeds

4. Standard, and simple graphical trading support

5. Visual representation of risk to the traders managing it.

IFR Forex Watch gives you real-time technical analysis of the FX spot and options markets. It gives you analysts in London, New York, Boston, San Francisco, Singapore and Sydney. Few can actually match the depth and variety that this program (International offers. IFR specializes in sifting through the vast array of Financing Review) information that clutters up current market participants, and boiling it down into its bare essentials.

Global Market Research provides price forecasting and is a proven performance-based Trade Strategies for the FX market trader. You should check out the daily newsletter, FX Technicals and intraday updates and analysis, through the Global Market Web or directly to your e-mail.

Research

This is a resource for a well-connected market professional that has been trading and writing about markets for nearly 20 years. You can capitalize off of his experience and his analysis, especially technical analysis, to get a real trader's take on current market action.

4CAST gives you key market information and analysis to market participants worldwide, including central banks. It also has an on-line service that gives you fundamental, political, strategic and technical analysis 24 hours a day.

ForexTRM is the only forex charting service that pairs 18 world and regional currencies and tracks them every day.

This means ForexTRM lets you to trade any one of the currencies against any of the other 17. It uses its unique trademarked Sigma Bands and Hurst Cycle Analysis to correctly identify:

• Overbought/sold forex markets

• Where trading risk is at its lowest point in time

• Which currency pairs are ready to trade

There is also an ALERTS Newsletter that you can get free of charge.

The Market Vu Show is the number one program for traders and active investors to use today. It lets you interact on your pc in real time as your host Market Vu and the famous Vu Team bring you live market action from the Global Forex Markets. It lets you watch professional traders and share ideas. You can also:

- Get Real Time Detailed Charts from the Vu Team
- Get LIVE Trade Setups, Entries, Stops and Profit

Targets

- Get Free Access for FX Account Holders

The Forex Edge is an instructional CD that tries to give Forex traders the unique tools that may just give them an advantage 50

to the rest of the field. It will show you how to identify unique formations and how to structure your own indicators and generate your own signals.

Here are a few more tools that you should check around for:

- Rate History Tool
- Converter
- EuroConverter
- Conversion List
- Risk Probability Calculator
- Investment Risks (VaR)
- Forex Pivot Point Calculator
- Pip USD value Calculator

As you can see, the buying and selling of currencies is necessary as it supports trade between countries in today's global marketplace and, as the major world currencies often work against one another, will continue to be. There is so much money to be made from currency transactions.

The major players in the market today are buying and selling in single deals and they are often running into many millions of dollars. The smaller players (as usual), like the brokerage houses and individual brokers, are often trading in single deals that consist of as little as one hundred thousand dollars.

Nowadays, you can join this market and, providing you take the time to learn everything that there is to know of the currency markets and have a little bit of capital to invest, you can have a great time and earn a very reasonable income from your trading efforts when you do it online.

As you have learned here you will not be able to trade on your own and will need to use a broker, but many brokers will allow you to open an account online and start trading with anywhere between $250 and $1,000. Many of them will let you try a free demo just to let you get the hang of it.

FOREX trading is not for everybody but its major advantage is that it is a highly liquid market that does not involve the commission payments and paperwork which many people find a problem like with other forms of trading. It is, however, a technical market and you should not try it unless you are absolutely ready to take the time to learn the basic principles that make up this currency market and become competent in the use of some of the tools at your disposal.

It is not necessary to become an expert in these markets to profit from them. With a little time and effort you can quite easily gain enough of an understanding of the currency markets to start making money online and off and, eventually you will be surprised at just how quickly you can become quite an expert.

The other factor here is using a trading system that actually works – without that, you're better off going to Vegas.

This guide has given you all of the knowledge you need to make money if you really want to. All you have to do is follow the advice mentioned here and do your research.

Next thing you know, you will be earning steady income from the forex trading market in no time at all!

Managing Your Money

When you start Forex trading, it is important to learn the basics of money management. If you just decide how much money you can afford to lose on a single trade, and start trading without any system, then you are not trading you are gambling. Forex trading is not about gambling and trying to win the jackpot, it is about making consistent profitable trades.

Unless you manage your money properly while trading the Forex, then you just as wel play the casinos in Las Vegas instead...

Some gamblers do make money in casinos, but many more people lose their money. The only people who consistently make a profit from gambling are the casino owners. Even when gamblers do win, the casino owners often bribe them with free hotel rooms, free food and drink etc. to carry on gambling, and in the end they lose al their money to the casino. When you trade the Forex, you need to think like the smart casino owner, not like a gambler...

And what if it was actually legit?

It's not a pipe dream. Literal y hundreds of traders are turning consistent, substantial profits each month just by running one program:

Forex Autopilot System (FAPS)

FAPS is our top-rated trading system on ForexShortcuts.com. And there's no reason why you can't start seeing massive results by riding the tailcoats of others' tried & true trading systems...

In any enterprise, it is always easier to lose money than to make it, and trading the Forex is no different.

For example, suppose you lose 50 percent of your bankroll on a trade. Now you have only 50 percent left to trade your way back to where you started. And what happens if you lose the other 50 percent on your next trade?

Gamblers often talk about winning streaks and losing streaks. When they think they are on to a winning streak they keep on staking al of their winnings on the next rol of the dice or spin of the roulette wheel –

and what happens? You've guessed it, they lose al their money, and end up broke. In Forex trading you can never rely on winning streaks, but losing streaks are a very real and ever present danger.

Suppose you have a trading system that returns a profit 70 percent of the time. You would expect 7 out of 10 trades to make a profit, and 3 out of 10 trades to make a loss. However this ratio is only true if you average out the results of hundreds or even thousands of trades. So if you make 100 trades, you wil probably make close to 70 profitable trades and 30 losing trades. But what if you start trading, and your first 10 trades are al losing trades?

The answer is you must only trade with a small percentage of your trading bankroll.

Forex: The World's Largest Financial Market

Forex is the world's biggest money related market, with over 5.09 trillion USD exchanged each and every day (April 2016). To place it at the end of the day, in a solitary day, more cash will be exchanged the Forex markets than Japan's whole GDP! (Total national output). Of these exchanges, 254 billion USD is exchanged through CFDs and other subordinate instruments.

Being the biggest, most dynamic monetary market on the globe, it is likewise the world's most fluid market, which means it is simple for dealers to go into, just as leave exchanges, and for the most fluid sets, they can do as such requiring little to no effort (even not exactly a solitary pip!). This additionally implies the Forex showcase is unstable, making numerous open doors for dealers to make a benefit on both the positive and negative developments of money sets.

Exchange Around the Clock

Forex is the one budgetary market that never rests, which means you can exchange at painfully inconvenient times of the day (or night). In contrast to the world's stock trades, which are situated in physical exchanging rooms like the New York Stock Exchange or the London Stock Exchange, the Forex showcase is known as an 'Over-the-counter market' (or OTC). This implies the exchanges happen straightforwardly between the gatherings holding the monetary standards, as opposed to being overseen through a trade.

Therefore, the Forex showcase has never been confined to the business hours of any one trade.

Nonetheless, since the Forex showcase is a worldwide market, it implies there is constantly a piece of the world that is wakeful and directing business, and during these hours their monetary standards will in general experience the most development. For instance, money sets including the US dollar experience the most development during US business hours (16:00 to 24:00 GMT), while the Euro, Pound, Swiss Franc and other European monetary standards experience the most development during European business hours, (8:00 and 16:00 GMT).

Paradoxically, the Australian Dollar, the New Zealand Dollar and the Japanese Yen will in general be increasingly dynamic somewhere in the range of 00:00 and 08:00 GMT. As a broker, this implies you can exchange at whatever point it suits you - in the event that you work during the day, there will be monetary standards accessible to exchange previously or after work. In the event that you have kids however are at home during the day, you can essentially pick an alternate cash. In the Forex advertise, you can exchange 24 hours per day, 5 days per week.

Guess on Rising or Falling Prices

One of the most widely recognized exchanging and speculation methods of reasoning is to 'purchase low and sell high' - this is especially the situation with long haul ventures, for example, putting resources into stocks or bonds, which depend on the benefit expanding in esteem. In the Forex showcase, you can likewise sell high and purchase low. Along these lines, you can conceivably make benefits on both descending and upward patterns.

As referenced before, in a long exchange (otherwise called a purchase exchange), a dealer will open an exchange at the offer cost, and will plan to close the exchange at a more significant expense, having a benefit on the effect between the opening and shutting estimation of the money pair. So if the EUR/USD offer value is 1.16667, and the exchange closes at the cost of 1.17568, the thing that matters is 0.00901, or 90.1 pips. (When exchanging a solitary part, that would make a 901 USD benefit).

Dealers can likewise make short exchanges (otherwise called sell exchanges), where they sell a Forex CFD at the ask cost and, when the value drops, get it at a lower offer cost, and benefit on the distinction. For this situation, if the GBP/USD ask cost was 1.32265, and the exchange shut at the cost of 1.31203, the distinction would be 0.01062, or 106.2 pips (which would add up to 1,062 USD in benefit).

Low Costs of Forex Trading

Due to Forex CFDs being utilized, brokers can get to huge parts of the cash advertise at an extremely low edge - now and again as low as 1/500th of the size of the market they need to get to (in view of an influence pace of 1:500). There are not many extra expenses also - most Forex exchanging accounts have pretty much nothing (or no) commissions, request charges, and record the board expenses. On the off chance that there are any exchanging expenses, these are typically a markup the intermediary has added to the spread.

Straightforward entry

Probably the best preferred position of Forex exchanging is that it is one of the most created monetary markets as far as innovation. While numerous business sectors are open by means of antiquated exchanging stages, there is consistent challenge as far as the product accessible for exchanging the FX advertise.

The stages offered by Admiral Markets incorporate MetaTrader 4 (MT4) and MetaTrader 5 (MT5) and MetaTrader WebTrader. MT4 and MT5 are both accessible for Windows, Mac, Android and iOS gadgets (for iPhone and iPad). What's more, Admiral Markets likewise furnishes dealers with an upgraded form of MetaTrader, known as MetaTrader Supreme Edition. With access to this product, Forex can be exchanged from anyplace on the planet - and all you need is a web association.

Exchanging With A Demo Account

Merchant's additionally can exchange chance free with a demo exchanging account. This implies merchants can abstain from putting their capital in danger, and they can pick when they wish to move to the live markets. For example, Admiral Markets' demo exchanging account empowers dealers to access the most recent continuous market information, the capacity to exchange with virtual cash, and access to the most recent exchanging bits of knowledge from master brokers.

7 Questions to Ask to Find the Right Forex Broker

With regards to picking a Forex representative, it can frequently feel like a mind-boggling decision, with incalculable choices accessible. Here are the top criteria you ought to think about when settling on your decision:

1. Is the specialist directed?

It may amaze you to discover that the Forex showcase doesn't have a focal controller. Notwithstanding, that doesn't mean you ought to pick a representative without thinking about the subject of guideline. Rather, we suggest picking a facilitate that is managed by the monetary controller in your general vicinity.

This would be the FCA (Financial Conduct Authority) in the UK, CySEC (Cyprus Securities and Exchange Commission) in Cyprus, ASIC (Australian Securities and Investments Commission) in Australia or SEC (Securities and Exchange Commission) in the US. A decent dealer will normally be glad for their authorizing and will utilize this as a selling point.

The advantage of picking a directed intermediary is that this will guarantee that you, as a broker, are ensured to the full degree of the law in your nation. For example, in 2018 the European Securities and Markets Authority (ESMA) presented a scope of enactment ensuring retail exchanging customers, which all European Forex agents must comply with. This enactment remembers limits for accessible influence, unpredictability security, negative equalization insurance and the sky is the limit from there.

It's likewise critical to think about the security of your assets. In view of this, we prescribe picking a facilitate that isolates their customers' assets from their own, which guarantees that the representative can't utilize your stores for any of their own monetary exercises.

It additionally guarantees that your assets will be accessible for withdrawal upon your solicitation. At long last, check whether the merchant offers a money related administrations remuneration conspire. This characterizes the measures of assets that will be remunerated to you in the extraordinary case that your agent or its bank is failing.

2. What is the nature of the agent's exchanging administration?

The administration of the specialist you pick, and the stage they offer, is fundamental in guaranteeing that you accomplish the best exchanging outcomes. On the off chance that you were exchanging on a framework that was moderate and consistently smashed, for instance, you probably won't have the option to enter or leave an exchange at the value you need. Rather, it's essential to search for an expedite that offers elevated levels of liquidity, low spreads and the capacity to execute orders at the value you need (or as near this as could be expected under the circumstances).

Another component of the administration gave is the edge necessities and level of influence accessible. While there is no compelling reason to pick the most significant level of accessible influence when you start exchanging Forex, just realizing that a dealer offers the most elevated level of influence endorsed by their controller implies that, as your experience develops, you can begin to expand your influence as per your inclinations.

3. What is the expense of exchanging?

As Forex exchanging can be a pay creating movement, it's critical to regard your exchanging as a business action - one where you think about both how to amplify your pay, how to limit your expenses, and how to limit the dangers. In light of this, try to consider the expenses of exchanging with any Forex specialist, before you at last select one.

Zones to consider include:

•	The size of their spreads: We've just talked about how the size of the spread impacts your potential exchanging benefits, as any cash pair needs to cross the spread before an exchange will get gainful. In light of this, search for a facilitate that offers low spreads.

•	Commissions: Ideally you ought to pick a Forex expedite that doesn't charge commissions, as commissions will cut into your potential benefits.

•	The least store: Many Forex specialists will request that dealers make a base store when opening a live exchanging record, so it is ideal to discover one with the most minimal measure of necessities. Chief naval officer Markets offers a base store of €200.

While looking for the least expensive Forex representative, it truly boils down to a blend of spreads, execution quality, commission, and the base store. These ought to be the last focuses you think about when opening a long haul exchanging account. The best Forex dealer for learners relies upon components like the exchanging framework, the statement feed, instrument portfolios, execution models, and the influence advertised.

4. What items and markets do they offer?

While picking a Forex intermediary, clearly you will need to ensure they approach a wide scope of cash sets, including majors, minors and exotics. In any case, shouldn't something be said about other money related instruments? In the event that you are thinking about exchanging with a Forex and CFD handle, it's a smart thought to investigate different instruments they offer too.

This will guarantee that in the event that you choose to exchange stocks, files, ETFs, items, cryptographic forms of money and different instruments later on, you won't have to locate another intermediary to do as such. Chief naval officer Markets, for instance, gives dealers access to more than 7,500 money related instruments, enabling you to make a differentiated exchanging and speculation methodology from a solitary stage.

5. Which exchanging apparatuses do they have accessible?

The nature of the exchanging instruments a Forex specialist offers can have a major effect to your exchanging experience. By and large, the accessible apparatuses will rely upon the exchanging stage (or stages) being utilized. For example, Admiral Markets offers exchanging through the cutting edge MetaTrader 4 and 5 Supreme Edition module, which incorporate a scope of custom devices and additional items to improve your exchanging experience.

6. Does the representative's offering suit your exchanging style?

It's essential to think about whether a Forex merchant and their exchanging stage will suit your exchanging style. For instance, you may be keen on following a Forex scalping methodology, which includes making a high volume of little benefits on little cash developments. For this situation, you would need to guarantee that any potential agent has least separation between the market cost and your stop-misfortune and take-benefit.

Or then again, on the off chance that you are new to Forex exchanging, you probably won't be open to utilizing the most extreme influence the intermediary offers. In view of this, check whether the merchant permits ostensible influence - where you can pick the measure of influence you use in your exchanging, anyplace up to as far as possible.

7. Do they offer training and backing?

At last, think about whether the Forex dealer offers instruction and backing. Continuous instruction is basic to a Forex broker's improvement and accomplishing the best outcomes. This is the reason Admiral Markets offers a scope of free articles and instructional exercises, online courses and online courses, including Forex 101 and Zero to Hero. Notwithstanding instructive substance and materials, it's additionally critical to think about the accessibility of help, so you can get your inquiries replied, and any potential issues managed.

Specifically, you should search for a Forex handle that has a significant nearness in your nation or, at any rate, offers telephone and email support in your language. A specialist with a proficient client enquiry and grumblings methodology will guarantee that if an enquiry is documented by a Forex broker and can't be settled inside a couple of hours, it is promptly sent to the client assistance work area or consistence office.

What to Look For in a Forex Trading Platform

Close by picking an intermediary, you will likewise be exploring the Forex exchanging programming and stages they offer. The exchanging stage is the focal component of your exchanging, and your fundamental working device. It is a basic bit of the riddle, as the best Forex devices can significantly affect your exchanging results. All in all, what would it be a good idea for you to search for while thinking about your alternatives?

While surveying a Forex exchanging stage, guarantee it incorporates the accompanying components:

• Reliability: Is the exchanging stage dependable enough for you to accomplish the exchanging results you need? Having the option to depend on the precision of costs cited, the speed of information being moved, and quick request execution is basic to having the option to exchange Forex effectively, especially on the off chance that you intend to utilize momentary techniques like scalping. The data must be accessible continuously, and the stage must be accessible consistently when the Forex advertise is open. This guarantees you can make the most of any open doors that may introduce themselves.

- Security: Will your assets and individual data be ensured? A respectable Forex merchant, and a decent Forex exchanging stage will have gauges set up to guarantee the security of your data, alongside the capacity to reinforcement all key record data. They will likewise isolate your assets from their very own assets. On the off chance that an intermediary can't show the measures they will take to ensure you and your record balance, it is ideal to locate another agent.

- Independent account the executives: Any Forex exchanging stage ought to enable you to deal with your exchanges and your record autonomously, without requesting that your dealer make a move for your benefit. This guarantees you can make a move when the market moves, profit by open doors as they emerge, and screen any open positions.

- Analysis: Does the stage give in-constructed examination?, or offer the devices for you to direct specialized and principal investigation freely? Numerous Forex merchants make exchanges dependent on specialized markers, and can exchange unquestionably more successfully in the event that they can get to this data inside the exchanging stage, instead of leaving the stage to discover it. This ought to incorporate graphs that are refreshed continuously, and access to forward-thinking market information and news.

•   Automated exchanging usefulness: One of the advantages of Forex exchanging is the capacity to open a position and set programmed stop misfortune and take benefit levels, at which the exchange will close. Progressively modern stages ought to have the usefulness to complete exchanging methodologies for your sake, when you have characterized the parameters for these systems. A decent exchanging stage will permit this degree of adaptability, as opposed to requiring a dealer to always be checking any exchanges.

At Admiral Markets, our foundation of decision are MetaTrader 4 and MetaTrader 5, which are the world's most easy to understand multi-resource exchanging stages. The two stages are open over a scope of gadgets including - PCs, Macs, iOS and Android gadgets and internet browsers through the MetaTrader Webtrader stage for MT4 and MT5. These are quick and responsive stages, giving constant exchanging information. Also, these stages offer robotized exchanging choices and progressed graphing abilities, and are profoundly secure.

MetaTrader 5, which is the latest rendition of the exchanging suite and has a scope of extra highlights, which include:

•   Access to a huge number of money related markets

•   An extended Mini Terminal, offering unlimited oversight of your record with a solitary snap

•   38 worked in exchanging pointers

•   The capacity to download tick history for a scope of instruments

•   Real volume exchanging information

•   Free advertise information, news and market training

•   Bonus exchanging gadgets with MetaTrader Supreme Edition

Would it be advisable for you to purchase Forex exchanging software?

While Forex exchanging for apprentices or experts will consistently require programming, the degree of rivalry between specialists implies that most Forex exchanging programming is accessible for nothing. Numerous Forex exchanging novices are likewise enticed to buy FX robots, otherwise called Expert Advisers (EAs). While a few EAs can be useful, it very well may be difficult for them to stay gainful when the market changes.

Except if you comprehend the code it's written in, you're presumably not going to have the option to adjust your EA to work with those changes. In the event that you are one of the numerous merchants who accept that an EA would outflank the market, at that point maybe you should try it out with the MetaTrader Supreme Edition module. What's more, maybe the best part is that we offer EAs for nothing out of pocket for merchants!

Step by step instructions to Manage Your Risk When Trading Forex

Before you make your first exchange, it's critical to think about how to viably deal with your hazard in the Forex advertise. As we've just talked about, exchanging Forex CFDs offers you the chance to exchange utilizing influence, which means you can utilize a generally little store to get to a bigger segment of the market (up to multiple times the estimation of your record balance, in case you're a Professional customer). This at that point increases your potential benefits to a similar degree. Be that as it may, it additionally increases your potential misfortunes.

To utilize an extraordinary model, envision holding a record parity of 2,000 EUR and putting the entirety of that on a solitary exchange. On the off chance that the exchange goes severely, you will have lost your whole venture, and on the grounds that the Forex market can move rapidly, misfortunes can likewise happen rapidly. This is the place chance administration is basic - to assist you with limiting misfortunes and ensure any benefits you do make. The key territories to think about when dealing with your Forex exchanging hazard are exchanging brain science, and cash the executives.

Ace Your Trading Psychology

While it may sound peculiar to talk about the themes of attitude and brain research in a manual for Forex exchanging, in all actuality these are probably the most significant variables isolating fruitful dealers from ineffective merchants.

Creating exchanging discipline and the capacity to deal with your feelings will assist you with staying cool under strain, entre exchanges at the opportune time, and to realize when to leave those exchanges - regardless of whether you are cutting your misfortunes, or taking your benefits before the market turns.

Some key exchanging brain research tips to remember include:

• Stay quiet: As energizing as exchanging can be, it is as yet upsetting work. There will be a great deal of difficulties on your way to the top. Feelings can pressure you to disclose more than what would have been prudent to open an exchange too soon as well as close it past the point of no return. The fundamental driver of worry for novices in exchanging is the way that some Forex exchanges will end in misfortune regardless – it's simply the manner in which the market is. Simply recall that war isn't won with a solitary fight. Or maybe, it is by and large execution that matters.

•   Understand your hazard resistance: Every individual has an alternate degree of hazard resilience, and this will impact the size of the odds they take, the misfortunes they are eager to encounter, and the mental impact of them. To deal with your feelings of anxiety while exchanging, it's essential to think about your degree of hazard resilience ahead of time, and pick exchanging procedures that help this.

For example, somebody with an okay resistance would be increasingly open to making loads of little exchanges after some time and giving the little benefits from each exchange a chance to include. On the other hand, somebody with a higher resistance for hazard would be all the more ready to make bigger exchanges, with the open doors for bigger increases (yet bigger misfortunes also).

•   Set reasonable exchanging objectives: It's critical to be sensible with your exchanging desires, as this will assist you with evaluating the best occasions to open and close exchanges. Numerous new Forex brokers have exceptionally elevated requirements about their potential benefits, and this makes them exchange forcefully, with huge aggregates of cash and quick choices. Once more, start little to test your insight and aptitudes, and as you start to dependably accomplish the outcomes you need, you can set greater objectives.

•	Set your cutoff points ahead of time: Before leaving on any Forex exchange, you ought to have characterized the cost at which you'll open the exchange, the cost at which you will close it and take your benefits, and the cost at which you will close it, should the market turn out of the blue, in this manner cutting your misfortunes. At that point, when you have set those limits, it's critical to stay with them!

Numerous new merchants decide not to close an exchange in light of the fact that the market is as yet moving toward the path they need it to, possibly to then lose the entirety of their increases when the course all of a sudden changes. In the event that your exchange hits your foreordained objective, close it and make the most of your rewards. On the off chance that the market moves the other way, close the exchange or set a stop misfortune so it will close naturally.

•	Prepare for the most noticeably awful: While this may sound negative, in Forex exchanging it is smarter to plan for the most exceedingly awful than anticipate the best. There have been ordinarily in history when budgetary markets and individual exchanging instruments have encountered unexpected spikes or drops in esteem. By thinking about the most noticeably awful conceivable result of an exchange, you can take measures to secure yourself, should this occur, for example, by setting a stop misfortune ahead of time.

Cash Management in Forex

Dealing with your cash in Forex exchanging comes down to the particular estimates you use to build your benefits, while likewise limiting potential misfortunes. Fruitful Forex exchanging has unmistakably more to do with powerful cash the executives than having a bunch of good exchanges, and is one of the privileged insights that isolates the individuals who effectively exchange FX over the long haul, from the individuals who surrender after a few exchanges.

For the minute however, here are some cash the executives basics to manage your exchanging:

•   Decide how you will back your exchanging advance: Only one sort of cash is useful for contributing, and that is the benevolent that you are eager to lose, and ideally without harming your physical or potentially mental prosperity all the while. Each productive dealer is gainful in their own particular manner, while each washout encounters misfortunes the very same way. Keep in mind, utilize each accessible chance to learn. It's an endless procedure!

•   Define your speculation level: One of the most widely recognized inquiries regarding exchanging Forex is 'what amount do I have to begin exchanging?' For apprentice brokers, it's a smart thought to begin little and stir your way up. Luckily, numerous Forex agents have sensible least store levels for opening a record. At Admiral Markets for instance, the base store sum is $200. Be careful about any agents offering rewards for certain store levels, as these may be tricks, where it is exceptionally hard to pull back your cash later on.

•   Calculate your hazard: Make sure to figure your hazard before you exchange. On the off chance that the potential benefits of an exchange are littler than the potential dangers, the exchange most likely is certainly not a decent choice. You can survey your hazard with our free Forex adding machine.

•   Determine the benefits required to cover any misfortunes: Along with ascertaining your dangers before any exchange, it's additionally worth figuring the amount you would need to make to recapture those assets in any future exchange. It's regularly harder to acquire cash back than it is to lose it, basically on the grounds that your outstanding venture pool is littler, which implies you need to make a bigger benefit (rate savvy) to equal the initial investment.

For instance, on the off chance that you contributed 5,000 EUR and lost 1,000 EUR, you will have lost 20% of your equalization, leaving you with a last parity of 4,000 EUR. To take your equalization back to 5,000 EUR, you should make a benefit of 1,000 EUR. Nonetheless, with a beginning equalization of 4,000 EUR (after the past misfortune), there is currently a 25% addition, instead of a 20% one.

- Start with little exchanges: To assist you with dealing with your hazard and save your capital, start by exchanging little entireties of cash, as opposed to going out on a limb with a huge segment of your record balance. For example, in the past model, in the event that you put your whole 2,000 EUR account balance on a solitary exchange, it is anything but difficult to lose everything.

On the other hand, on the off chance that you just exchanged 20 EUR, a misfortune would not essentially influence your record balance. It would give you the chance to gain from your experience and plan your next exchange all the more successfully. In view of this, restricting the capital you are set up to hazard to 5% of your record equalization (or lower) will place you in a superior situation to keep exchanging Forex (and improving your method) over the long haul.

Hazard Management Tools and Techniques

When you have aced your exchanging brain research and cash the executives, there are various exchanging procedures you can apply to additionally diminish your hazard:

•   Diversify your portfolio: We all know the maxim, 'don't place all your investments tied up on one place', yet numerous new FX dealers do this with regards to their exchanging. Similarly as it isn't savvy to place the entirety of your assets into a solitary exchange, depending on a solitary cash pair builds your degree of hazard, supposing that the pair moves an alternate way to what you expect, you could lose everything. Rather, consider opening various little exchanges crosswise over various Forex sets.

You could even consider exchanging other CFD instruments also, for example, shares, files, wares, cryptographic forms of money and that's just the beginning, as these will additionally enhance your exchanging portfolio.

•   Use influence astutely: As we've just referenced, Forex CFDs enable you to exchange on an edge, or by utilizing influence. Notwithstanding, in light of the fact that 1:30 (or 1:500) influence is accessible, it doesn't imply that you have to utilize it. At Admiral

Markets, while there is a most extreme measure of influence accessible to our customers, they are as yet ready to pick the measure of influence they use when they are exchanging, which might be anything up to that sum.

For example, in the wake of surveying your hazard, you may choose that the potential expenses of exchanging with a 1:30 degree of influence are excessively incredible, and you are progressively alright with 1:5. Picking a lower ostensible influence will assist you with managing your hazard viably, particularly in the event that you are new to Forex exchanging.

•   Focus on the long haul: The underlying phases of your exchanging ought to be tied in with protecting your capital – making an effort not to develop it. Limiting danger is the essential target. One approach to perhaps accomplish this is by using a long haul exchanging position.

What easygoing Forex exchanging amateurs frequently neglect to acknowledge is that the best dealers attempt to make an arrival on their venture dependent on long haul patterns. They frequently hold their requests open for quite a long time, months and even a very long time at once. Thusly, Forex functions as a venture as opposed to a lottery.

- Use a stop misfortune: A stop misfortune is device that merchants use to confine their potential misfortunes. Basically, it is the value level at which you will close an exchange that isn't moving in support of you, in this way counteracting any further misfortunes as the market keeps on moving toward that path. You can likewise utilize a stop misfortune to monitor any benefits you may have just made - the device to accomplish this is known as a 'trailing' stop misfortune, which pursues the course of the market.

For example, in the event that you opened a long exchange on the GBP/USD cash pair, and the pair expanded in esteem, as far as possible at which the exchange should close (the stop misfortune) would move nearby the cost of the money pair. In the event that the estimation of the GBP/USD then began to fall, the exchange would be shut when it hit your stop misfortune, safeguarding any benefits you had made heretofore.

- Continue your Forex instruction: The business sectors are continually changing, with new exchanging thoughts and techniques being distributed normally. To guarantee you keep on building up your exchanging aptitudes, it's imperative to remain over your exchanging training by consistently looking into advertise investigation and by adapting new exchanging procedures. For all the more exchanging training, investigate our

Forex and CFD online classes, which are intended to develop your insight as you begin and keep on exchanging.

How to Analyse the Forex Market

While some new Forex traders might experience beginner's luck, and open a trade on the right currency pair in the right direction, this luck rarely lasts. For long-term trading success, a trader needs to be able to make informed trading decisions, and these decisions are a result of analysing the market.

Analysis is absolutely vital to trading. Charts are helpful for both short and long-term trading. You should be looking at daily, weekly, and monthly charts. Fortunately, there are a number of different approaches to Forex analysis, which means every trader can find the right approach for them. The three broad categories of Forex analysis are fundamental analysis, technical analysis and wave analysis.

Fundamental Analysis

This form of analysis involves look keeping track of real-world events that might influence the values of the financial instruments you want to trade. For instance, the value of the Australian Dollar might fluctuate following a Reserve Bank of

Australia interest rate announcement, which will then affect the movements of all currency pairs including the AUD.

The seven economic indicators that have the greatest impact on the Forex market are:

• Gross domestic product (GDP)

• The number of jobs outside the agricultural sector (known as Non-Farm Payrolls, or NFP)

• The rate of unemployment

• The index of industrial production

• Retail sales

• Orders for durable goods

• The interest rates of national banks (such as the European Central Bank or the US Federal Reserve)

There are then three possible scenarios following an economic publication or announcement:

1. No reaction, implying that the market had anticipated the announcement

2. A strong movement in accordance with the economic data that has been made public (so if the announcement shares positive news, the instrument affected by this news will increase in value)

3. A strong movement against the economic data shared

The challenge is assessing which outcome is the most likely, and then opening a trade accordingly. A good starting point for this trading approach is first being aware of upcoming events that may affect the Forex market (refer to our live Forex calendar for the latest events) and second, looking at the effect similar announcements had on different currency pairs in the past. You can learn more about fundamental analysis in our Introduction to Fundamental Analysis article.

Technical Analysis

While fundamental analysis focuses on what is happening in the real world, including economic, political, and business news and events, technical analysis largely focuses on what is happening in trading charts.

Trading charts simply chronicle the price movements of different trading instruments over time, which allows traders to identify patterns in price movements and make trading decisions based on the assumption that these patterns will repeat in the future. For example, one trading chart format is the Japanese candlestick chart, which is formatted to emphasise high and low price points for certain time increments (these increments can be set by the trader in their trading platform).

The trader can then see:

- The opening price for the period

- The highest price point for the period

- The lowest price point for the period

- The closing price for the period

This information can then allow traders to make judgements regarding a currency pair's price movement. For example, if a Japanese candlestick closes near the highest price for the period, that would imply that there is a strong interest on the part of buyers for this currency pair during that time period. A trader might then decide to open a long trade to take advantage of that interest.

Over time, common patterns emerge in the movement of the charts (and the formation of different candlesticks), which can then be used to predict potential future price movements and make the best trades based on these predictions.

Once a pattern emerges, this is known as a Forex indicator because it indicates that there is the potential to make a profitable trade. While there are a range of resources available online for learning about the best Forex indicators, your trading software should ideally have a range of built-in indicators that you can use for your trading, as is the case with MetaTrader 5's indicators. You can learn more about technical analysis in our Introduction to Technical Analysis article.

Wave Analysis

Wave analysis, also known as Elliott Wave analysis, is a well-known method that analyses the price chart for patterns and the direction (trend) of a financial instrument. The method is based on historical movements in market prices, with the belief that history repeats itself. The reason for this is due to market sentiment, meaning that the market as a whole moves as a herd, and reacts in a similar way to similar events and announcements.

In the Forex market, these reactions involve buying and selling currencies, which causes the prices of different currency pairs to fluctuate.

The theory follows sequences of five waves, or five up and down price movements which are then countered by a corrective 3 wave pattern in the opposite direction. The 5 impulsive waves are with the trend, whereas the 3 corrective waves are counter trend. In an 'up' move, there will be three up waves (movements 1, 3 and 5) and two down waves (movements 2 and 4).

In a corrective down move, there will be 2 waves down (A and C) and 1 wave up (B). In a down move, the instrument will make 3 waves down which are separated by 2 waves up. The corrective up wave will have 2 waves up and 1 wave down. Following this, the instrument will make a 'down' move, with three down waves being separated by two up waves.

While this pattern does not take place every time prices move, traders can use this method as a guideline for whether or not to enter into or exit a trade by taking the following steps:

1. Determine how you will generate the Elliott Wave count, keeping in mind that the approach must be consistent for all 'up' and 'down' movements.

2. Wait for a wave to begin. In many cases it is wise to wait until the end of the third or the beginning of the fourth movement in the wave, to ensure that the instrument is following the Elliott Wave price pattern.

3. Use a secondary indicator (or indicators) to confirm the trend.

Once you have taken these steps, you can enter into a trade with more confidence. If you would like to learn more about wave analysis, please read our Introduction to Forex Elliott Wave Analysis article.

6 Popular Forex Strategies

Now you know the what, the why, and the how of Forex trading. The next step to to create a trading strategy. For beginner traders, the ideal scenario is to follow a simple and effective strategy, which will allow you to confirm what works and what doesn't work, without too many variables confusing things. Fortunately, banks, corporations, investors, and speculators have all been trading the markets for decades, which means there is already a wide range of Forex trading strategies to choose from. These include:

• Forex scalping: Scalping is a trading strategy that involves buying and selling currency pairs in very short increments - usually anywhere between a few seconds and a few hours. This is a very hands-on strategy that involves making a large number of small profits until those profits add up.

• Intraday trading: Forex intraday trading is a more conservative approach than scalping, with trades focusing on daily price trends. Trades may be open anywhere between one to four days, but usually focus on the major sessions for each Forex market.

• Swing trading: Swing trading is a medium-term trading approach that focuses on larger price movements than scalping or intraday trading. This means that traders can set up a trade and check in on it within a few hours, or a few days, rather than having to constantly sit in front of their trading platform, making it a good option for people trading alongside a day job.

• Forex hedging: Hedging is a risk management technique where a trader can offset potential losses by taking opposite positions in the market. In Forex, this can be done by taking two opposite positions on the same currency pair (e.g. by opening a long trade and a short trade on the GBP/USD currency pair), or by taking opposite positions on two correlated currencies.

• The Forex martingale strategy: The martingale strategy is a trading strategy whereby, for every losing trade, you double the investment made in future trades in order to recover your losses, as soon as you make a successful trade. For instance, if you invest 1 EUR on your first trade and lose, on the next trade you would invest 2 EUR, then 4 EUR , then 8 EUR and so on. Please note that this strategy is extremely risky by nature and not suitable for beginners!

• The Forex grid strategy: The grid strategy is one that uses buy stop orders and sell stop orders to profit on natural market movements. These orders are usually placed at 10 pip intervals and, by having these stop orders put in place, a trader can then automate this trading strategy.

TYPES OF FINANCIAL MARKETS

Markets generally are classified by type. The capital markets consist of the stock and bond markets, which have instruments that may be traded on the New York Stock Exchange (NYSE). There are also commodities and derivatives markets, which feature financial products that are based on the underlying commodities and are traded on central exchanges such as the Chicago Mercantile Exchange. The markets on which this book will focus are the financial markets, the foreign exchange market, or forex, in particular.

Risk versus Reward

Before beginning an investing or trading program, it is very important to understand the concept of risk versus reward. All investments carry some degree of risk; there is no such thing as a zero-risk investment. Higher potential rewards almost always are coupled with higher risk. The markets this book will cover are considered a high-risk investment. We do not recommend a high-risk investment strategy for any money you cannot afford to lose. Risk can include factors, such as inflation and recessions, that affect the value of what you are holding.

Methods That Apply to Multiple Markets

The methods we will be discussing apply to all markets, including stocks, bonds, futures, options, and forex. Because of the liquidity of the international currency markets, the low cost of entry, and the advent of easy-to-use platforms and free charting packages, along with mini and micro contracts, most of the examples we give will be in the forex markets.

Foreign Currency Trading

Foreign currency trading on a retail level was the brainchild of Leo Melamed, chairman emeritus of the Chicago Mercantile Exchange, with encouragement from the economist and Nobel laureate Milton Friedman. In 1972 the Chicago Mercantile Exchange started trading futures that were based on the exchange rate between the U.S. dollar and other major currencies, and the growth in financial derivatives has not slowed since that time.

Foreign exchange trading was nothing new to banks and large institutions, and it wasn't long before brokers and dealers around the world devised ways to make markets outside the central location of the futures market in Chicago. The name forex is an abbreviation for the words "foreign exchange." Worldwide, the forex market is the most actively traded financial market. The daily volume on the forex market is equal to three to four times that of all other markets combined, with an average daily turnover of $3.2 trillion. Forex is an extremely liquid market because of the high level of participation, or high volume, and the fact that currencies have a tendency to move in sustained trends relative to other markets or investments. Liquidity is important if one wants to be able to get in and out of a market quickly, and when we study trending markets, you will see that strong trends represent opportunities to make a lot of money if you are on the right side of the trade. Forex is traded 24 hours a day during the workweek, closing Friday at 5 p.m. Eastern Standard Time and reopening Sunday at 5 p.m. Forex also has a low cost of entry; an investor can open an account with as little as $250.

Currency Trading History

Here are the highlights of the history of currency trading.

• When currency systems were introduced, a country's currency value was set against a gold standard.

• In times of rapid political and economic change, the gold standard becomes a problem. Therefore, after World War I and

World War II, many countries abandoned the gold standard and adopted the Bretton Woods Accord.

• Between 1944 and 1971, exchange rates for foreign currencies were set at a price fixed against the U.S. dollar.

• In December 1971, the Bretton Woods Accord that had established the fixed rates was abandoned, and several other systems were implemented briefly before a floating exchange system was established.

• In 1972, the Chicago Mercantile Exchange starting trading currency futures.

• At present, the currencies of most countries are valued relative to the value of other currencies.

• With the expansion of the World Wide Web, the forex market has been opened to include speculators and private investors.

Forex versus Futures

For professional investors, there are a couple of distinct advantages to trading currency futures contracts. First, traders who use currency futures are assured that their funds are placed in a bank account segregated from the dealing firm's money; this is different from the practice of many foreign exchange dealers, in which the client's and the dealer's money often are commingled. Futures also ensure lower transactions costs because the markup between the bid and the offer is determined by professional traders and market makers who participate in the transparent and very competitive world of futures trading, not by individual banks and dealers who generally mark up the spread to wider levels. It is through this spread that forex dealers are compensated. Although forex dealers have had to respond with tighter spreads for their clients over the last year or so, these advantages still generally lie with futures markets: Futures still maintain a tighter spread between the bid and the offer, and futures clients have negotiated their commission to well below the minimum tick value that represents the smallest increment in which the price can move.

On any given day the Chicago Mercantile Exchange (CME) trades over 400,000 currency futures contracts for a face value of over

$400 billion in business. However, because of larger account minimums, larger contract sizes, higher margin rates, and government regulations, the futures markets have taken a backseat to the growth of the underregulated cash currency markets, or forex, over the last 10 years. In futures markets, traders compete among themselves and with market makers around the clock, with all the participants having access to the same tight bid and offer, or spread, that is created in a central marketplace regulated by the National Futures Association, whereas traders in forex compete directly with the dealer. The dealer shows the client what is known as a retail spread, whereas the dealer has excess to an institutional spread and the futures spread, which are generally tighter than the retail forex spread. This difference between the retail spread and the institutional spread is profitable for forex dealers, particularly since a high percentage of the participants trading with the dealer are not professionals. Having this distinct advantage, along with the Internet to promote their services, dealers spend a good percentage of their profits on upgrading their state-of-the-art trading platforms and charting packages to entice clients to trade with them.

These efforts by the dealers to improve their order delivery platforms and charting and analysis packages can benefit educated clients. Another advantage for clients who choose to trade with a forex dealer is the smaller contract sizes. One of the main reasons retail clients lose money trading is that they risk too much per transaction. In futures the minimum contract size is $62,500, whereas in forex it is just $1,000 for a micro contract and $10,000 for a mini contract. With these smaller contracts, it is much easier for a retail client to manage and maintain acceptable trading risk-reward ratios than it would be with the larger futures contracts. Because of the ease of trade management the smaller forex contracts afford, particularly the fact that a trader can keep the risk per trade to a fixed percentage of his or her account size, we will focus primarily on the forex markets. If you are inexperienced in trading, especially in trading forex, keep in mind that it is a very serious business. The dealers are in business to capture the transactional costs generated by your trading. You are in business to make money trading. You need to understand this duality: Information you receive directly or indirectly from a dealer is geared toward getting you to trade more to generate the transactional costs created by the spread.

CONCLUSION

We have covered a lot of information in this article so, we'd like to conclude with an overview of our top Forex trading tips for beginners. If you take anything from this book, it should be these following tips:

Forex Basics

As we mentioned previously, the forex market is traded 24 hours a day during the workweek and closes on Friday at 5 p.m. EST.

The hours are adjusted in the United States during Daylight Savings Time.

What Is Traded on Forex?

Almost all the transactions on the forex market involve currency pairs. However, it is possible to trade precious metals through most foreign exchange dealers.

The Six Majors

The most commonly traded currency pairs on the forex market are called the six majors. They are the British pound (GBPUSD, also known as "sterling" or the "cable"), the Canadian dollar (USDCAD, aka the "looney"), the Australian dollar (AUDUSD, aka the "Aussie"), the Japanese yen (USDJPY, aka the "yen"), the euro (EURUSD, aka the "fiber"), and the Swiss franc (USDCHF, aka the "Swissy" or "chief").

Distribution by Currency Pair

It is estimated that the U.S. dollar is involved in over 70 percent of all transactions on the forex markets. Figure 1-4 shows the breakdown of volume traded for the major currency pairs.

Cross Currency Pairs

Cross currency pairs are those which do not involve the U.S. dollar. They tend to trade at lower volume, and the spreads are usually higher for these pairs than for the 7majors. An exception to this rule are pairs such as the euroyen (EURJPY) and euro swiss (EURCHF), which offer tight spreads and excellent trading opportunities. Examples of cross currency pairs include Canadian dollar/Japanese yen // CADJPY, New Zealand dollar/Japanese yen // NZDJPY, euro/Japanese yen // EURJPY, and British pound/Japanese yen // GBPJPY. We will discuss in more detail the contribution of the major currencies to the global marketplace.

Understanding Currency Pairs

Currency prices are quoted relative to another currency's price as a result of constantly fluctuating values. In each currency 9 pair, the first currency listed is the base currency and always has a value of 1.0. The second currency listed is the counter currency. For example, EURUSD is the value of the euro expressed in U.S. dollars.

Understanding Currency Values

The following example shows how fluctuations affect currency prices:

- USD/JPY 110.08 means that 1 U.S. dollar equals 110.08 Japanese yen.

- If the price moves to USD/JPY 111.08, it means that the dollar has gotten stronger, as one could buy more yen per dollar.

- Conversely, if the price moves to USD/JPY 109.08, the dollar has gotten weaker, as it buys fewer yen per dollar.

- Prices for the JPY are given to two decimal places, but prices for all other currencies are given to four decimal places.

What Is a Pip?

A pip is the smallest value by which a currency may fluctuate in the forex market. Pip stands for "price in percentage" and sometimes is referred to as a "tick." Let us see how this works.

- A move from EUR/USD 1.5555 to 1.5550 is referred to as a 5-pip move.

- A move from USD/JPY 113.00 to 113.05 also is referred to as a 5-pip move, since the yen is recorded only out to two decimal places.

It is a good idea to do the math and know what a pip equates to in terms of the base currency one is trading. For most scenarios, the pip is equal to 0.0001, or 0.01 percent.

Lot Sizes

A standard currency contract is referred to as a lot. Initially, lot sizes were very large because currencies were traded only by large financial institutions. As the "retail" sector of the forex market opened up, the market came up with smaller units called mini lots and micro lots. Figure 1-9 lists their values.

With the advent of smaller lot sizes, the market has been opened up to a larger number of individuals.

The ask price is the price at which a trader will buy the base currency in exchange for the counter currency. The bid price is the price at which a trader will sell the base currency in exchange for the counter currency. The bid price is always lower than the ask price. Figure 1-10 shows how the bid and ask prices equal the spread.

The Spread

The spread is the difference between the bid price and the ask price. Figure 1-11 shows how the spread is calculated.

The spread is the compensation a broker receives for every transaction an investor places. Spreads are usually fairly

"tight" for the major currency pairs, but they can be considerably higher for cross currency pairs. This is one reason we do not recommend trading cross currency pairs except in a long-term position trade; the costs may be too high to make it consistently profitable.

Understanding Leverage

Leverage is the factor that makes forex trading both high-risk and high-reward. You put up only a portion of the amount traded and then can trade up to 200 times the value of your account. With leverage, the total value of your account can increase faster and also can be wiped out much faster. Start slowly with leverage and then move up your ratios slowly as you gain experience. We will talk about this concept in the section on money management. A limited number of brokers also offer leverage of up to 400 times the value of an account. We do not recommend ever using that much leverage. You do not want to risk more than the value of your account; for the most part there are no margin calls, and the broker will close out all your positions to avoid incurring a debit balance. You can lose your entire account very quickly if it is highly leveraged.

Although some dealers and forex brokers give their clients assurances that they cannot lose more money than they have in the account, if there is a cataclysmic event, those assurances may not hold up. It is crucial that you understand risk and follow the rules necessary to limit your downside risk. Many errors in forex are due to failure to follow the established rules.

Margin Calls

When your account has leverage, the total dollar value of the currency you control is much larger than the value of your account. For example, if you have an account that is leveraged 200:1, a $1,000 balance controls $200,000 worth of currency.

Your account is worth 1/200, or one-half of a percent, of the contract you control. That means that if the underlying currency moves by 0.5 percent and you are on the wrong side of the move, your account value will go down to zero.

Conversely, if you are on the right side of the move and the currency moves to the same degree, your account value will double. It is a double-edged sword. If your account value falls to zero, the broker or dealer will try to close out your position to avoid a debit balance. In other financial markets the practice has been for the broker to make a call to the customer to see if the customer would like to put up extra margin to stay in his or her position, hoping that things will turn around. Our philosophy on margins calls is "never answer a margin call," and with most forex brokers you don't have a choice. They try to close your position out for you before the account goes into debit. If they do not close it out in time, however, you will incur the debt.

Minimizing Risk

We talk in greater detail about minimizing risk in the section on money management. Before you get started, though, there are some basic rules about risk that you need to know and observe:

• We recommend practicing with a demo account before trading a "live" account.

• Develop your confidence and skills on a demo account or micro account, and once you have developed a good track record, switch to a live account.

- Always monitor your positions actively.

- Never hold a position without an accompanying stop-loss order. This is an order that is based on how much you are willing to risk on the trade. If you have a 200-pip stop order, once the trade moves 200 pips against you, the position is closed automatically.

- Never risk more than 5 percent of the value of your account on one transaction.

- Have a trading plan that outlines your entry and exit strategies. We will show you how to build a trading plan.

- Follow your trading plan.

Do Your Research

Generally speaking, the less you know, the more at risk you are, and there is no limit to how much you can know or risk. An endless amount of information is available on the internet free of charge, like:

- Educational videos on Forex exchange trading for beginners

- Educational articles and tutorials

- Forex trading seminars for beginners and professionals

- Forex trading webinars

If you want to know how to learn Forex trading as a beginner, simply read as much as you possibly can, and always analyse what you read – don't just take information in good faith.

Test on a Demo Account or With Simulation Software

Every broker offers a demo account – whether you are a beginner or not, test every new strategy there first. Keep going until the results are conclusive and you are confident in what you are testing. Only then should you open a live account and use your strategy in the smallest volume trades available. Be sure to treat your demo account trades as if they were real trades. You may also use Forex simulation software to simulate market conditions, and create an impression of a live trading session.

Don't Overcomplicate Things

Don't overload your charts with indicators, or your strategy with handles or switches. The more complicated your trading strategy is, the harder it will be to follow, and the less likely it is to be effective. To find out how well a strategy performs on average in different markets, you need to carry out the necessary backtesting and research.

Keeping it simple can be a real challenge, especially considering the multitude of supporting tools you can apply to your charts. Just remember – it's not about the amount of tools at your disposal, but it is about being able to use a few tools in an effective way.

Be Careful in Volatile Markets

Volatility is what keeps your trading activity moving. However, if you're not careful it can also completely destroy it. When volatile, the market moves sideways, which makes spreads grow and your orders slip. As a beginner Forex trader, you need to accept that once you are in the market, anything can potentially happen, and it can completely negate your strategy.

For example, the crisis with the Swiss Franc in January 2015 ended business for many traders and brokers within hours of its occurrence. Admiral Markets have helped to minimise volatility risk for you by offering a package of advanced volatility trading settings to help you avoid the reefs of the financial markets.

The Trend Is Your Friend

Whether you are a beginner trader or a pro, it is best to trade with what you see and not what you think. For example, you might think that the US dollar is overvalued and has been overvalued for too long. Naturally, you will want to short and you might be right eventually. But if the price is moving up, it does not matter what you think. In fact, it doesn't matter what anybody thinks – the price is moving up and you should be trading with the trend.

The Trade Is Open Until It's Closed

A regular Forex trading beginner concentrates on opening a trade, but the exit point is equally important. If your trading strategy does not consider the mechanism of closing a deal, it's not going to end well, and you're much more likely to suffer heavy losses.

Write Everything Down

A novice Forex trader must develop the mindset of a business owner. Every business requires a business plan, constant monitoring, and regular auditing. Jumping ahead without plans and processes is a sure-fire way to fail. Starting a trading journal is an absolute must.

Everyday, be sure to write the following:

- Points for further research

- Reasons to open or close a trade

- Your achievements and mistakes

Keep your journal handy as a point of reference when analysing your activity. A journal ensures none of your actions are in vain. Analysis of good trades will boost your trading confidence and motivate you to push harder and go further. On the other hand, analysis of bad trades will help you to extract value and improve.

Forex Trading With Admiral Markets

If you're aiming to take your trading to the next level, the Admiral Markets live account is the perfect place for you to do that! Trade Forex & CFDs on 80+ currencies, choosing from a range of Forex majors, Forex minors, and exotic currency pairs, with access to the latest technical analysis and trading information.

www.ingramcontent.com/pod-product-compliance
Lightning Source LLC
Chambersburg PA
CBHW070643220526
45466CB00001B/277